LIKE IT WAS

By the same author:

LIKE IT WAS

JAMES KOLLER

BLACKBERRY BOOKS

Text ©1999 James Koller
Photos ©1999 Zoe Brown
ISBN: 0-942396-84-7

Sections of this book have been previously published
as follows:

"The Autobiography" was included as part of "Fifty
Years," *Contemporary Authors*, Volume 5, Gale
Research Co., Detroit; 1985.

Poems were originally published in *California Poems*,
Black Sparrow, Los Angeles, 1971; *O Didn't He
Ramble*, Coyote & Bussard, Ferndale, Washington &
Schwetzingen BRD, 1980; *A Gang of Four*, Coyote's
Journal, Brunswick, Maine, 1989.

Sections of "The Spirits With Us Now," along with
other sections of the novel *I Went To See My True Love*
were included in The Cafe Review, Portland, Maine,
1991.

Cover art is from an untitled painting by Jack Boyce.

This book was published by
Blackberry Books
617 East Neck Road
Nobleboro, Maine 04555

Contents

"..that place no longer exists."
Philip Whalen

History & One's Past

This book represents a collection drawn from published autobiographical material, from my own poetry previously published in English and French, and from my unpublished third novel. All the material included here was written during, or is about, the period generally referred to as Sixties San Francisco.

My purpose in making the selection I have was to make it possible for readers to consider the variety of ways in which even a single author might deal with what we like to call "the facts."

While writing from my own life, knowing all the facts of that life, I have, I realize, seldom represented the events and particulars of that life ("the facts") with the same eye from genre to genre. I have rather tried to let each genre inform the work – with each allowing its own freedoms and limitations. While a memoir is generally written with an eye to what other participants in the same events might consider the history of the time, neither poetry nor fiction are so limited, and it will be seen that in them I have followed my own fancy, while still attempting to keep the flavor of the work consistent with my overall intent as an artist.

To the degree that my approach is not unique, it offers a view of practices well beyond my own, and so, I'd hope, a better understanding of the creative process.

It should be noted that those who haven't lived in a period are likely to have fewer misgivings about writings from that period than those who have. Such readers must necessarily take more for granted, and unless they are serious students of the period, will seldom fully appreciate the inconsistencies of a time's histories.

A major problem for those without their own memories of a time or place is that a history they might read often misrepresents the ideas and motives of that time and place even where incontrovertible recorded facts remain consistent. This is especially true of history written from the ideological present.

Writing remembered history from the perspective of the present is in essence rewriting history. Values that were once mainstream are no longer, and writing of them as we see them in the present is to give rise to radical misrepresentations of what they were in the past. In 1960 there was a labor movement trying to improve working conditions; women were not afforded anything like an equal status with men in any area; Afro American, Hispanic, Asian or American Indian civil rights were not acknowledged as a problem; there was an unpopular military draft of those young men who were unable to manipulate the facts of their lives; much of America feared communism, did believe that any war to stop it was just. We assume today that all of these conditions are phenomena of the past. To fully understand history we must watch it pass. The pieces in this collection appear as written, a product of their own time.

November 1999

From The Autobiography (1985)

It is said today that we invent ourselves. We pick from all that is offered those things that make up what we come to think of as ourselves. Some believe that it makes sense to afford one's self as many possibilities as one can - see as much, know as much. Others see life as a very simple thing, where what really matters is shown to nearly all. The way it seems to work is that you learn the simple things after you've tried everything else.

Those who people one's life contribute their input into that life – they too have a heavy hand in inventing you, as they imagine you, and as you play off that image. As you change, or think you want to change, you find yourself meeting new people, making new friends, who will reenforce those changes, allow you to see yourself as you want to be seen. You retain those friends who see you as you want to be.

When one remembers, the sensations, feelings, thoughts, pass again, a *remembered now*, that one carries into all nows. Past becomes present. Old friends, living and dead, people one's now. The dead die only as those who knew them forget or die themselves. To visit old friends is to bring into the now all past nows – to wake and create a continued and expanded common now. It is one's life and one must keep it all alive or one begins to die.

The Years 1956-1973

In the summer of '56 I drove west first to Seattle and Puyallup, where friends of my folks from Illinois owned an orchard, and then down the coast to south-

9

ern Oregon, where a friend from college, Lyndon Viel, was working at the Oregon Caves National Monument as a bus driver. I found work in the kitchen for a month, then continued down the coast to San Francisco, where I discovered City Lights Bookstore. The city was filled with energy and I felt it but couldn't connect. After a week I continued on down the coast to Long Beach, then inland into the Sierras, back to Monterey, and back to Cave Junction, up old Highway 99, where late at night in the Siskiyous I'm sure I saw a big old wolf waiting beside the road for a chance to cross. I worked again, long enough to buy four tires, and Lyndon and I drove back to Wisconsin, to Monroe, on two-lane roads, in forty-seven hours and fifty-three minutes. Traveling alone I read a lot – what I remember was Sandburg's *Complete Poems*, Dos Passos' *U.S.A.*, and Steinbeck's *Grapes of Wrath*.

Though Jean Rada and I were from neighboring towns, we went to different high schools and did not meet until we shared classes at North Central College (Naperville, Illinois). We began dating in the fall of '56 and were married in the summer of '57, between our junior and senior years. We traveled to Quebec City for our honeymoon, then down the Maine coast and back to Illinois, moving to a converted chicken house in a town close to the college, where we resumed our studies, both of us in English and Drama. I read reviews of Kerouac's *On The Road* in the fall of '57 and ordered the book. The same reviews turned me to those people referred to as the San Francisco Poets, who were said to be in league with Kerouac. I ordered Ferlinghetti's *Coney Island of the Mind* when word of it reached me. I bought *Evergreen Review, No. 2*. I tried to interest others in this work but had little luck. Jean and I traveled to San Francisco in the summer of '58, spent two weeks exploring the city from a cheap room on Ellis or Eddy Street before we returned to Illinois, where I expected to be drafted. I wasn't, and Jean taught school for a year. I wrote what became Brainard and Washington Street Poems, read all of Pound, chasing down all the references I could, which led me into Chinese and French poetry. With the college close at hand I was able to direct a presentation of Beckett's *Endgame*, which Jean acted in. We spent the summer of '59 traveling around the country, doing museums and art shows (Jean painted) and bookstores in NYC and Boston (where I was introduced to Zen, by Alan Watts, on TV), camping in British Columbia (where one night we sat so quietly a bear didn't realize we were there until he was right next to us), and finally, walking and walking through San Francisco.

In the fall of '59 I enrolled at the University of Iowa, and Jean signed on with the Iowa City school system. I was there only a short time before I realized I was in the wrong place. On the first day of classes I met Marlene and Michael Fine. When I dropped out of the University in November, Jean and I helped Marlene and Michael open their bookstore, the Paper Place, the first all-paperback store between NYC and San Francisco. A friend in San Francisco, Carl Marcoux, who had gone to college with us, discovered Auerhahn Press, and sent us word of their new books as they appeared. (The first we saw was John Weiner's *Hotel Wentley Poems*, then Michael McClure's *Hymns to Saint Geryon* and Philip Whalen's *Memoirs of an Interglacial Age*.) My first reading was in a coffee house above the bookstore. In May, Jean and I left for San Francisco, arrived the day Francis Powers and his U-2 were shot down. I spent the summer working part-time at the Tides Bookstore in Sausalito, started full-time warehouse work with Paper Editions Corporation the day after our daughter, Deirdre, was born – August 21, 1960. I talked about blues and folk music for months with the Apache kid who worked with me. We lived on Hyde Street, 1317, third floor, walked up. We shared the place with Carl Marcoux, who introduced us to Bill and Laura Kwong, who lived a block away. Bill was just getting into Zen, and we talked a lot about Buddhism, Zen. A cable line ran in front of the apartment and we took the cable car or walked most everywhere we went. One day while I was walking home from work, on Fourth Street, near the train station, a black man, thinking me a wino, offered me fifty cents to help carry his laundry. I did, and waited outside while he went in to get me my money.

While in Iowa I sent my writings to *Evergreen Review*. Irving Rosenthal responded, arranging a meeting with Don Allen in San Francisco, soon after I arrived. Don introduced me to Michael McClure, who lived above a garage, painted huge blue paintings, and was just beginning to write plays. We talked a lot of Blake. Don introduced me to Philip Whalen at McClure's reading of his *Dark Brown*. Philip had read some of the work I had given Don, work from *Two Hands*, and told me I clearly had to write. I told him I would get better. Don also introduced me to Richard Brautigan and Richard Duerden.

In March '61 we went back to Illinois. Jean and Deirdre flew from San Francisco, and I drove down to L.A., where I visited Jim Smith, another college friend, whose path has crossed mine again and again since we first met in '54. I drove from L.A. nonstop to Iowa City, to visit Michael and Marlene Fine, and a few hours after I arrived, ended up driving Michael on to Chicago, an all night drive in fog, to get him to a train connection which he had to make for his induction into the U.S. Army. I worked for Paper Editions Corporation in Chicago, on West Jackson, from the spring into the fall, reading Henry Miller (Parisian editions of the *Tropic of Cancer*, and *Tropic of Capricorn*, gifts from Michael Fine) on the way to and from work, on the commuter trains between Chicago and Naperville, where we lived in a small house south of town. We spent a lot of time in these months with Pam and Fred Millward, whom we had known in college. We all wrote, had all studied with Richard Eastman. One night in April, Millwards came for dinner and were snowed in in a sudden and heavy storm. Snow plows totally buried their car where they left it beside the road to walk back after finding it impossible to return home. The snow was almost totally gone the next night. In summer, electrical storms made electricity jump across the rooms from wall outlet to wall outlet. Hemingway killed himself that summer and I painted a huge black painting in the front yard. At the end of summer we decided to go west again.

Smith had moved from L.A. to Seattle, and we headed to Seattle, thinking to go on to San Francisco if no work turned up. We stayed in Seattle nearly a year. Smith worked for Hartman's, a large bookstore near the University of Washington, a bookstore owned by the same man who owned Paper Editions. I found work as paperback buyer. Jean gave me an Alaskan Malamute puppy for Christmas. The dog was a female and we bought her on an arrangement which provided that we were to breed her and give pick of the litter to her former owner. We ended up with several dogs. In March of '62 I started work for Warshal's Sporting Goods, inventorying their several outlets, carrying merchandise from the main store to the outlets. In the fall Jean went back to teaching, in Burlington, and we moved to Bow. I took care of my daughter, my dogs, and my garden. I wandered around in the mountains below Baker and Shuksan, and when there wasn't money to go that far, or the old Chevy wouldn't run well enough, I was on Chuckanut Mountain. I wrote lots of letters, a novel (*Shannon, Who Was Lost Before*), and two books of poems (*The Dogs and Other Dark Woods* and *Some Cows, Poems of Civilization and Domestic Life*). Don Allen sent out many of my poems to magazines and it was through his efforts that the first of my poems were published. In '63, after the Vancouver Conference, Philip Whalen wrote me and suggested I try some of my work with the *Northwest Review* in Eugene, Oregon. He had met Ed Van Aelstyn, who edited the magazine, in Vancouver. I wrote Ed, sent him work, and discovered his poetry editor was leaving. I suggested I could do the job and Ed put me on. The University suspended publication of the Review in '64 because of extreme reaction to an issue which contained work by Whalen, Antonin Artaud, and an interview with Fidel Castro. Van Aelstyn, Will Wroth and I decided to begin a magazine, initially to publish those works we'd accepted for publication in the *Northwest Review*. *Coyote's Journal* began, branched almost immediately into book publication. Most of the work was done by mail, but we did meet together, made more than one fast trip together to the Bay Area. I met Bill Brown and his wife Zoe and daughter Maggie, and Joanne Kyger, who had just returned from Japan, on one such a trip. Another time there was a benefit for *Coyote's Journal* and *Wild Dog* at Fugazi Hall. As I prepared to leave on one of these trips, I said goodbye to Jean, then looked for

Deirdre. She was nowhere to be found. After looking for some time, I discovered her behind the seat in the car, stowed away. Christmas of '64, Jean and Deirdre and I drove down to Everett, took the train back to Illinois. We heard the Paul Butterfield Blues Band at Big John's in Chicago. In the spring of '65 we drove down to California to check out job possibilities for Jean, and she landed a job in San Rafael, at more than twice the wage she made in Washington. When her school year ended, we drove once more to Illinois, then back, to move. *Two Hands* was published as we made ready.

Jean stayed behind in Bellingham, did summer work at the University, and Deirdre and I drove down to San Francisco, the four-wheeled trailer hauling all of our belongings behind us. Coming over Siskiyou Pass the brakes overheated and we were without brakes on the two-lane road, cars swerving quickly in front us in the face of oncoming traffic and there was no way with automatic transmission to slow down. We finally stopped in Yreka by dragging the trailer wheels against a long empty curb and waited until the brakes came back.

We found a house to rent in San Rafael on D Street, near where Jean would teach and Deirdre begin school. There was a huge oak in the back yard, a bed of Naked Ladies against the back wall. I began *California Poems* at the kitchen table, listening to D Street traffic. Dick Baker, who had worked with me at Paper Editions, invited me to read at the opening reading of the Berkeley Poetry Conference. Bob Creeley introduced me. I attended very few of the lectures and readings, but managed to meet Drum Hadley, Charles Olson, and many others. I got to know Bill Brown and he suggested I help him clear up the field where his new house in Bolinas would be built. When we were finished he offered me a job, gardening and landscaping, which I took. My first recollection of Jack Boyce, who was living then with Joanne Kyger in San Francisco, was of him breaking up concrete with a maul and pick. Soon after meeting Jack, I had dinner one night with him and Joanne at their place on Pine Street. After too much alcohol and too many cigars I found myself in the bathroom being sick. I don't know how long I was in there, but Joanne eventually asked if I would like a pillow.

I first met Bill Deemer in Eugene, in '64, when he read with Ronald Johnson and myself. In '65 Bill lived in San Francisco, in a small room in a building where Max Finstein also lived. Bill and his sweetheart, Toby, and I went for dinner one night in Chinatown, met up with Philip Whalen, who came with us. We all ate with chopsticks from the same large bowl and we all hurried to keep up with Philip but we didn't stand a chance. Billy and Toby had an apartment on Fell Street, opposite the Panhandle, when they were married across the street in the park in March '66. I spent hours that day talking to Patsy Zoline, who had grown up in Chicago, who had graduated from the University of Chicago, and had been a graduate student in philosophy at Stanford. Zoline lived on Duboce Street with several others, including Karl Bruder, and it was there that I met Neal Cassady, who passed through while I was having a quiet dinner with Z.

Jack and Joanne were married in the summer of '66. We partied afterwards at the Doss house in San Francisco, a party that included champagne without end and dancing – at one point a circle dance ended with all falling to the floor. When the party ended Joanne waited on the curb while Jack carried out some cardboard cases of champagne. The case bottoms were wet and the bottles began to fall one after the other and several exploded before Jack finally realized what was happening. They went home to find their place on Pine Street filled with rice – their bed, every pot, every drawer – and Jack collected it, filled a one hundred-pound bag, which they later ate. There were many parties, many at Brown's in Bolinas, where many of us often spent our Sundays, Bill talking as he worked in his garden. One Sunday Jack introduced me to Kirby Doyle, who he had once worked with him in Big Sur, packing tons of cement bag by bag up trails to a building site.

In the fall of '66, after her second summer in Bellingham, Jean moved with Deirdre to an apartment in San Rafael and I to a house in Sebastopol. We lived apart for several months, then tried again and lived together in Sebastopol until we separated in mid-'67. I met Elizabeth Baker at a party at Muir Beach while she was visiting California. We wrote and arranged my coming to Detroit, where she lived. On my way I stayed briefly in Aspen with Patsy Zoline and had the luck of meeting Paul Blackburn, Robert Vas Dias and Bobby Byrd. Paul and I became friends immediately and talked at length of his translations from the Provençal, which he loaned to me in manuscript. Blackburn, of all my contemporaries, seemed to have learned the most from Pound. From Aspen I moved on to the riots in Detroit, where Elizabeth and I lay all night on the floor listening to the sounds of machine guns and rifle fire and screeching wheels and sirens. The television gave us instant coverage. The entire upper Midwest seemed under siege.

After a return to Illinois to help my cousin Curtis move his furnishings and farm animals (I remember trying to catch the ducks), Elizabeth, her son, Ben, who was three, and I traveled east. Jack and Joanne traveled in Europe for the six months following their wedding, then settled into a loft in NYC for another six months. Elizabeth and I arrived in New York in late summer. Jack and Joanne introduced us to many of their new friends, and then arranged for us to return in a few weeks, when we would all travel together back to California, which we did, all their things in the back of the pickup as far as Jack's mother's in Michigan, Jack and Thomas Thomas (the one Malamute I had kept) riding in the back with them. In Michigan we rented a trailer, so some might ride in the covered bed. We drove from Michigan to Wyoming, Yellowstone, and then to the Northwest. Jack shot movies of the trip. Somewhere in the Northwest, driving late at night looking for a place to park, Jack and I decided to head on home. The ladies slept through the night and in the morning found themselves far from where they expected to be. I again stayed at Brown's, worked with him. Elizabeth and Ben headed for Aspen, where they would settle.

I put Elizabeth on the bus in San Francisco the morning of September 21, 1967. I spent the afternoon with Patsy Zoline and Michael and Joanne McClure. That night, Cass Finley, whom Richard Brautigan had once brought to Brown's, and who was visiting now on her own, climbed the ladder to my loft. Cass grew up in New Jersey, outside of Philadelphia, started college in North Carolina, was married briefly, spent the next year in Philadelphia, and had flown to San Francisco in early '67, where she quickly met Brautigan, Peter Coyote, and the Diggers. After months in the city she traveled with others to New Mexico, where she had hoped to settle, and had returned to the city for what she had thought would be a short visit. She stayed on with me, and a few weeks later we drove to El Rito to pick up her belongings. When we returned we found a small house to rent on Sparkes Road in Sebastopol, the house where I wrote the screenplay for *If You Don't Like Me You Can Leave Me Alone*, and all but the last poem in the second section of *California Poems*.

We spent much of the time I wasn't working in San Francisco visiting Lenore Kandel and Billy Fritch, Peter Coyote and Sam, Peter and Judy Berg, and others of the Diggers – who then were at the peak of their activity. The Diggers functioned first as a community, then as social movers and shakers, focused much of the seemingly disparate energy running rampant on Haight Street. They staged many events, provided many people with a sense of community that has only been paralleled in my life by the poetic community, which Cass and I stayed a part of. I met Franco Beltrametti when I picked him up at Philip Whalen's suggestion at the pier where his ship came in from Japan, where Philip was and had met him. When Philip returned I met his ship, and moved his belongings from place to place. We visited often with Jack and Joanne, in Bodega (just around the corner from where I had once visited Brautigan), in the little blue house in San Francisco (where Lewis and Phoebe MacAdams, Tom and Angelica Clark, Lewis Warsh and Anne Waldman came when they came west, and where I got to know them, and where I introduced Jack to Patsy Zoline; a house which she and I once almost rented), and later in Bolinas when they lived in the yurt on the land where Jack would build his house. When Gary Snyder returned from Japan with Masa, we met the boat, visited often before the Snyders moved to the Ridge. I first met Lew Welch at Philip Whalen's 123 Beaver Street apartment in '65, but never really knew him well before he too came to know the Diggers.

Drum Hadley hitchhiked up from Arizona in the summer of '68; I remember that the Datura were in bloom where we walked under the apple trees. There were many late-night visitors, coming in from far and wide, off the road. I was reading Eliade's *Shamanism* and it found an easy place in most conversations.

When Brautigan learned that Cass was pregnant he wanted to know where she had conceived and was disappointed when he learned it had happened in bed. Our daughter, Jessie Aldebaran, was born in the Sparkes Road house, November 21, 1968. Sam, who was like a sister then to Cass, had come in a few days earlier from Colorado, to be there for the birth. Peter Coyote was in Olema, and I drove early that morning to get him, so that he might be there. Five weeks later, on the same winding back road, I was struck by a Volkswagen, out of control on the wet road, the woman driving thrown from her car and killed. While waiting for an insurance settlement, we traveled east by train, to Chicago and New Jersey, to show off the grandchild. We were gone a month, spent time in NYC with Lewis and Anne and Ted Berrigan and others. When we returned we bought a '62 Chevy Travelall, cut our belongings to what would fit and gave up our house, using Olema as our home base. We went first to Idaho and Montana, spent many weeks there, parking on the sides of logging roads, watching the melting snow seep into the ground. After a short return we went on to Tucson, and the Hadleys, stayed for weeks, in town and at Dart Ranch in the Chiricahuas where Drum first showed me the life of a cowboy.

The summer of '69 we were back in Olema with Peter Coyote. Deirdre spent a month with us, the four of us living out of the back of the truck. My folks came to visit, stayed at a motel in San Rafael. Before going to visit them, Cass and I walked into a local department store and the head cashier ordered all the others to close their drawers when she saw us – Bonnie and Clyde fresh in her mind.

In September '69 we headed north again, saw Deemers in Oregon, then headed east to Chicago, New Jersey, and then to Mountain Dale, New York, arriving a few weeks after Woodstock. We spent several weeks exploring the fields and woods and made periodic trips to NYC. We were harassed by the police, who connected us to the others wandering the countryside. For Thanksgiving we drove to Savannah, Georgia, to visit a cousin Cass had grown up with, my first visit to the south in nineteen years. Somehow I had expected that it alone had not changed – would be as I remembered it. I was wrong. We spent December in Illinois, I skinning mink with Curtis, who raised them, living again out of the truck.

On Christmas day we headed south for Santa Fe, where Hadleys had just bought a house. We spent a few nights with them, then drove on to Olema, Bolinas, and San Francisco, to collect those belongings we'd left behind, and were back in Santa Fe by the end of January, where we rented part of a house on Camino Del Monte Sol. We lived there until fall. I rewrote *Shannon*, expanded *If You Don't Like Me You Can Leave Me Alone* into a novel, finished *California Poems*, wrote *Wind, Fragments for a Beginning*. I worked as well at carpentry and general construction with Tony Martinez, then at masonry with Felipe Gabaldon. Through Hadleys we came to know Keith and Eloise Wilson and Mona Sakiestewa, and through Mona many more, Jerome Rothenberg among them. Peter Coyote, Jack, Bill Brown, Lew Welch and Magda, and many others came to visit. Snyders and Nanao Sakaki came to Hadleys and I first met Nanao then, visited again with Allen Ginsberg, in that house on Monte Sol, which reminded him of one Ed Dorn had once lived in in Santa Fe. Deirdre was with us for a month that summer, and Jessie and I took her back to California, leaving Cass, who had found work, behind. The truck broke down several times going and coming, and though I drove straight through coming back, it took days. In the fall the landlord wanted the house for his daughter and we were forced to move. We stayed for awhile with Mona, then found a house on Garcia, around the corner from Hadleys. I had to clean and paint the whole house. In late December I helped Mona drive to Woodstock, where her first husband-to-be lived. Except for an overnight with friends in Kansas City we drove straight through, arrived at dawn, the ground covered with deep snow, the temperature twenty-five below. I returned by train, train wrecks all through the Midwest, and I was routed far out of my way. When I returned, I found that it was over between Cass and me. I spent three weeks putting things in order before I left for San Francisco. The night before I left, there was a big poetry reading to benefit Black Mesa, and I came to know Peg Swift, who organized the reading, that night. I met Simon Ortiz at Hadley's the next morning, where he had come to visit Gary Snyder who was staying there. I gave Simon a ride when I left, towards Albuquerque.

I was in California about six weeks. I went first to Olema, arrived at Coyote's as the last of the bikers straggled out after a party that had lasted for days. I learned that a caravan was forming and that Peter was going to move on, move out of Olema. I went on to Bolinas, and somehow Jack and I ended up going to

Petaluma where we spent several days putting together a fence. Nights we hit the bars in towns nearby and talked a lot of other bars. Jack told of how he and Lew Welch got kicked out of every bar from Gazelle to Grants Pass when they lived in the Siskiyou. Bill Brown was living with Wilma and others north of Bolinas, truck farming, and I slept nights there in my truck,or at Jack's, when Jack and I returned to Bolinas. Jack and Joanne were no longer together. Patsy Zoline was expecting Jack's baby, though she and Jack couldn't stand to live together – Lynne O'Hare and her children lived with Jack in the house he was building. My copy of *California Poems* arrived in the mail and I went up to Olema to show it to Peter, and found Peter and a small group finishing up their moving, and we all stood around drinking and I read the last poem in the book to those there, before we all left together.

I went back to Santa Fe. I picked up a hitchhiker in San Bernadino, an ex-marine who had first seen duty in the Detroit riots, had shot a man as he climbed out of the bus in his hometown. We compared notes and decided there was ample reason to believe that the riots had been incited. As we drove into Williams in the middle of the night we were stopped by a roadblock, twenty or so men with rifles standing behind parked police cars. They were looking for someone who had robbed a restaurant, checked my arm for a telltale tattoo which wasn't there and we drove on. I left the ex-marine in Albuquerque, he was on his way home, and I drove north toward Santa Fe, and lost my fuel pump. Mona came to my rescue. I spent the next few days at Hadleys, looked up Peg Swift.

Peg Swift – Marguerite, after her mother – had lived in the Southwest for several years before I met her, mostly on the Navajo Reservation, mostly working as a journalist. She was born in NYC, spent her early years in Connecticut and summers for many years afterwards in Maine. She had lived and traveled extensively in Europe and the Middle East, in Mexico and Central America. In April '71 she was housesitting in Santa Fe, writing free-lance. After a two week courtship we drove to Maine to visit her father who was dying. We were there most of May. Otis Swift had spent his early days in the newspaper world, as a writer, and then in Depression years got into public relations. He had lived well a life of his own choosing. He died in June, we were gone, back to the Southwest on our way to California where I was to have done a reading which we found had been canceled. We traveled for several weeks with Deirdre and Jessie, back to Illinois, and then west again to take the girls home. We visited Peter Coyote, the caravan nearly ready. I worked in Petaluma, built a deck, and Peg went off each day to San Francisco, where she catalogued material for Julia Newman's Tenth Muse. In late September '71 I saw Jack for the last time. Patsy's baby had died at birth, Jack had gone to southern Mexico for several months. We talked of Lew Welch's disappearance – Jack had spent days helping in the search for his body, which was never found and which Jack hoped meant that he might be still alive. We watched Jack's movies.

Peg and I headed east to Illinois. We built a sixteen-by-sixteen-foot cabin in six weeks on my Aunt Laura's land, a half mile from the road, on a wooded creek that ran through the property. We built the cabin of scrap wood, salvaged wood and a bucket of nails from a barn that had burned down. The farm dump was close at hand and we found everything there we needed. The place cost, including the stove with a bad bottom, thirty-five dollars. We lived there through the winter, Jessie with us for six weeks. I began *Bureau Creek*, wrote "Message in My Poems." Peg left in March to help her mother return to Maine. I followed in May, after editing and annotating Peg's *Winter in the Illinois Woods*. After readings in Chicago I headed east, where we stayed for several months in Wayne, Maine in a house loaned to us by Douglas MacDonald, on the shores of Lake Androscoggin. Gary Lawless introduced himself and Ted Enslin and arranged several readings in Maine for Ted and myself. Peter and Judy Berg visited, and Peter Coyote was best man at our wedding in June '72, up from Pennsylvania where he'd come after his father died.

In August I went to NYC to work with Michael Fine, who had sold the Paper Place in Iowa years earlier and had returned to New York, and who now was beginning Bookthrift, a remainder company. I stayed with Michael and Marlene weekdays, drove to Maine for the weekends. It was on one of those long weekends in Maine that Lewis MacAdams called to tell me that Jack Boyce was dead. A few hours later Bill Brown and Patsy Zoline called. Jack died September 30, 1972, he was forty. He fell from a beam in his house, struck his head on a cast-iron stove. He was cremated, his ashes somewhere on Mount Tamalpais.

In October '72 Peg decided to move down to NYC too. The apartment was on Bank Street, right around the corner from the White Horse Tavern. We lived together in the city until Christmas, when Peg moved back to Maine. I stayed on in the city through February '73 back at Fines', Maine on weekends, until I went west in March trying to generate interest in Bookthrift. I was gone for two months. I drove through Wyoming, Colorado, New Mexico, Arizona, California as far north as Sacramento, and Nevada. Most of my time

25

was spent in university towns. I hit a lot of bad weather, was snowed in briefly in Laramie and northern Colorado, hit bad ice near Flagstaff. I spent time with Wilsons, Hadleys, and Mona in the Southwest, with everyone I knew in California. Peter Coyote and I drove back together from San Francisco to Pennsylvania, where I left him, drove on to NYC, then to Maine.

Peg was pregnant. We decided to leave the East, move to Colorado. We packed everything into a trailer and drove to Morrison, stayed with old friends while we looked for a place to rent and work. We were there only a few days when I fell and broke both wrists – June 10, 1973. We bought a tent and camped for the next month, while my wrists began mending, then too restless to stay longer, I drove to New Mexico, picked up Jessie, drove to California, where I picked up Deirdre. The three of us drove to Spokane, Peg flew up to meet us. We wandered, camping, over western Montana, Idaho, Washington, and Oregon for several weeks, then drove back to California, dropped Deirdre off, and drove back to New Mexico, where after taking Jessie home we camped another two weeks while we decided what to do next. My hands were still not fully operative – I couldn't do any heavy lifting. We decided to pick up our things in Colorado and return to Maine. We did.

Jedediah was born in Brunswick, Maine, November 23, 1973. The apartment we rented was in a building which had once been a hospital and now catered to mostly navy people. Many of the women who lived in the building were pregnant or had just had a child. Peter Coyote parked his trailer in the back yard that Christmas.

THE POEMS
(1965-76)

This selection is dedicated to
Bill Brown, Jack Boyce, Franco Beltrametti,
Richard Brautigan & Lew Welch,
on the other side

THAT FALL, ON BICYCLE, AT DUSK,
                    I heard the Canadian Geese –
honking, low over the Samish, out the mouth
south, after the sun

    & winter was early & hard

driving to Bothell, the seminary lawn
covered with coots

    my daughter woke me with a flute

off San Rafael Creek, the bay – today – full of coots

    I saw a girl in Burlington
    with a wild goose
    blazoned on the back of her jacket

       she was going to the bowling alley

I was driving my truck home from the dump

RADIO POEM

Wiggle Yr Toes Chew

(Eve, of Destruction)

somebody else singing yr song, again

contemplation

falling stars

WHOOSH BOOM

Hey, Red! Yeah, yeah. Ride.

Going my way?

Hey, Red, yeah – wiggle

someone to know me
someone to throw me

EEHAA!!!

choose yr partner, split lady split
wiggle chew

WHOOSH BANG!!!!!

(I'll be here. Don't ask why.
Won't tell anybody.
My feelings are hurt.
Sonumbitch.)

show me the valley - show me the trail

(devastation)

You & I. Merry-go-round
all yoops loops the loops
        HOOPLA!!!

((A Public Service Message:

        whatever it is you have in yr mouth -))

everybody is singing yr song

                        (NEWS! NEWS! THE ANTS
                        are in yr underwear.

                        what are they after?

                        come, come)

whatever, whatever

        raw red frayed tongue yr hands
        ain't making
        any headway

"Baby, Laugh At Me, & I'll Cry For You"

Do you want an apple?
I'll take off my shoes.

I'M GOING HOME!

---

                you forgot
your raincoat
I'm bringing it, I'm
coming home

        leave my potatoes, oranges
        toilet paper & peanuts

(I haven't shit in the woods since 56 – Smith
    a roll of toilet paper, a red flag, in hand)

going home, the rain

        so hard the wipers shorted out,
        the horn stuck, the ignition wouldn't turn off

        piss on a flat rock

                when god was a little boy

                        a gray squirrel
                        top of a fence post

        leave one rifle, 16 shells, 2 maps
            the rifle a Remington, bolt, 30-06
            the shells Winchester, same caliber
            the maps, Liberty & Mt. Stuart, 15', 1961

            a nuthatch nearly lit on my shoulder

another on the gun barrel

he had a green bill

coming down, off Shuksan
dark, alone
I almost shot a porcupine

thought he was a bear

(Sandy Dances in Eugene, white fringe
Louie Louie, If I Had A Hammer)

you win, you win

see you another day

going home

the rings are chrome
if they don't seat by 5,000
complain

"this ain't no original"

we ate lunch
Someplace
a dead salmon
awash at our feet

the white pup, like a Samoyed
want to buy him?
took him in trade, thought
I could sell him

cars, people on foot, Snoqualmie Pass
the mountain goat like a patch of leftover snow

oak for heat
fir for kindling, cooking

"those are leaves burning"

the girl in the laundromat, Seattle
black net stockings
a hole just below her left knee

the leaves falling, blowing away
we walked the early morning streets
empty except for us &
the giant orange streetcleaners

(David or Andrew, Rebecca Ann
who you gonna be, Smith baby?)

hail in with the rain

in Eugene, drove the wrong way down a one-way
the officer, when he saw California plates
Washington driver's license

Where DO you live??

I'M *GOING* HOME

you win you win

"every time you come, I get pains in my belly"

gas

Wolf Creek, Weed, & Maxwell

How's Thomas?
        Fine.
How do you know?
        I'm here with him.

Hang on, Sloopy.

I ain't no Shanshiro Sugata
   smiling in my sleep –
the crazy one taking his knife from my throat
   chewing his nails in fear

      "I'm in on something –
         this ain't no one night stand!"

      but my eyes are open

why do you walk so fast?

  a lope
    (can't walk a straight line
      unless I walk fast)

  the secret is out

"It's a heavy load –
   they all are"

    put in hot water, a toilet
     Kyoto, settling in

       an old roommate returning

I bought another bottle
(visitors from the north)
Inventory: 1 gallon red wine – Paisano
        11 12 oz. bottles of beer – Budweiser
        1/5 gallon sake – Koshu

1/5 gallon bourbon – Jack Daniels
1/5 gallon rye – Old Overholt
(Ed & Carole, Vanny, Paula, Nico & Philip)
    settling in

& tea:
        Darjeeling, Lapsang Suchong, Oolong, Gen-mai

    all cups full

the wolf looks after his family

    I'm looking

        wind warnings in the Siskiyou
        snow down to 2,000 feet in the Sierra
        nine inches of rain San Bernadino County
            where one & a half is usual
            floods, slides

        all is not usual

IT ALL HAS TO DO WITH THE ANIMAL –
THE MEAT BLOOD BONE & HAIR
IT'S ALL THERE – THE IMPACT

        whether or not we touch –
        I mean I don't have to touch you
        to know you are there

    "There is a weapon in the room"

TO KNOW
    you only have to be there

groves of cedar, fir, oak – rock – running or standing
water – mountains, plains, river valleys –
snow & rain – the sun

you only have to be there

flowers opening in your head

I ain't the mother of any civilization
(the father of one girl-child –
but you have to start somewhere)

I don't know anything until I get there

"thin-chested?"

"WOLF MAN!"

I was always a gray wolf
like Pere Vidal of Old

looking after the chickens

save your silver bullets

I lope
in loops – circles
(miles & miles – but circles)
LE LOUP
like the "white bear"
sometimes a grizzly phenomenon

IF MY HEART IS WITH YOU

it is because you were here
   with me

               (I felt her heart
              the pounding
              in the ground
              in the bottoms of my feet)

you know or you don't
   it's like that
& you do or you don't
   like that
            settle in

how did you know?
   my totem?

CANIS LUPIS
           didn't know it showed

SO EARLY TO WAKE – DARK
& it has been a night of rain
I was surprised when the sun came – the rain gone
& like your gown, the camellias
fallen to the ground

THE BLACKBERRIES WERE NOT RIPE
but we found two, nearly ready, not green
ate them

wrapped together, out of the wind
the gull put down over us,
or so it seemed looking back
as we did, the side of the bluff, shale
rolling chunks & scree

the air was different

I was not to be found & you waited
found you, on the bed, the blanket, alone

we walked back, all
up hill, dust

he told me you were like a daughter to him

go easy, slow
I have a bad ankle

BLUE GREEN A MOUNTAIN LAKE THE SKY
clear above
young red plum leaves, blossoms
snow on wet river stones

I came to you, you asked that I come
I wanted to, would have, come anyway

your tears, my tears

all day I listen to crows

the ground warm a warm rain

tears, the blue green a dress &
skin, wet river stones, tears

plum blossoms

crows, the sky

I hold you
someday you are going away

POEM FOR YELLOW HAIR

who did you come with, you asked
caw caw caw

                        high into the trees
I think I was too drunk to answer

yellow light & all the greens
yellow
            after the rain
grass & willows
out my window
& the apple trees in blossom

maybe time to know each other

I don't know why I came
(not answering your question)

I followed the crows
(not answering your question)

on the beach
or in the mountains
maybe time
a few good moments

if you get to where you're going
                                    (follow

the crows)
I'll be there

the horses fat from apples

POEM FOR JACK BOYCE

We smoked cigars, watched.
Beer cans in hand, our ladies danced
squat & peed on the moonlit road.
I don't remember what kind of cigars they were
only that they cost one dollar apiece,
that we saved the butts, smoked them
planting trees the next day.

for Ed Van Aelstyn

"SORRY, LADY, THE TRAIN JUST LEFT 10 MINUTES AGO"
a long time going a long time gone

– a ticket to ride –

somebody stole my radio / I'm tuning in elsewhere
(the phonograph has a short in the arm)
a shot in the arm?
(the "H' train? "hard stuff"? NO! HARRIET!)

Venus Contaminated

the picture was of three wolves
a back shot, the ears, tipped, plainly visible
north of the Brooks Range –

I'm homesick, have never been there

with the advent of summer

the priest with his foot covering someone else's
dropped winning race ticket

travelers all

the secret: unequal portions, the balance in time
nothing comes apart in the same way
something always

on its way

just a question of what goes first
he'd told them not to go to Madrid –

Franco was still in power, but they went
    & the night they were to arrive
he went to see a movie on the Spanish Civil War
       the dead in the Basque country
       the dead in Guernica
       the dead in Madrid

    TO DIE IN MADRID

three wolves

    MUSSOLINI TOLD THEM THAT IF THEY
    WEREN'T VICTORIOUS HE'D KILL THEM,
    HIS OWN SOLDIERS

        his wife says she was just a homebody

the sun today woke me
& later there was rain & wind
Snow – March 1st 1966 – Westshore Drive, Belvedere
        & on Mt. Tamalpais

the convict returned on his own
three nights alone in the Marin hills

they named the creeks after themselves
   John & Bill Sochor
ALYESHKA, the Russians called it

      contaminated, the Americans said
(they weren't – the Americans weren't – first)

it becomes a matter of selection, whether
    you want it bad enough

(fighting wars is just a way out)

everything in unequal portions
            mountains & valleys or
                        a little of everything: fish, fowl, meat

                        & don't forget the vegetables
                        brush with soft butter
                        SPRINKLE WITH SALT

THE DOOR NEITHER OPEN NOR CLOSED

                        & now Harriet
                        more demand than supply, he said

whether you want *what* bad enough??

marriage is an institution

            three days in the Marin hills & he returned

IN UNEQUAL PROPORTIONS

take what you get give what you like

                        there ain't
                        no balance just
                        pulsation – wheels
                        they were

she wasn't making it with just anybody
            she was making it with me

TO DIE ANYWHERE

like I said
home sick
I never been there

they just keep cutting out

If anything really wild happens, let me know.

IT HAPPENS ALL THE TIME.

*

VENUS IS A PLANET WHERE THE RUSSIANS
STARTED LIFE TODAY

THERE ARE STILL THREE WOLVES NORTH
OF THE BROOKS RANGE
IN ALASKA, WHERE THE RUSSIANS ALSO
SENT SHIPS

& WHAT DID THE RUSSIANS HAVE TO DO
WITH SPAIN, YOU ASK?

*

it's been over an hour since that train left

I WENT TO SEE MY TRUE LOVE

at twelve, midnight, I started north
Stinson to Olema, twenty minutes
one deer before Bolinas

    Nobody's Child, dressed in black
    (Mary & Child, a postcard, behind her head)

    a bottle of vodka, can of V8
    didn't drink any

early evening, another night, same road
I saw half a dozen deer

     it was not an immaculate conception

blinking lights on the false front
jukebox music, laughter
drifting up the road
somebody twenty minutes in the phonebooth
before he walked, flashlight in his hand, up the hill

this is my scene * don't bug me * &c.

   it was very nice of you to come get this for her

    thoughtful kind brave clean & reverent

     what about cheerful

you're awful to do this for me

watched her dress, hair down, hair up, hair down

to the liquor store, deliver her
to somebody else

on the first day I saw her
we knew
everybody did. All the others

so where are you now???

everybody

the thing to use, he said, is a shotgun
one shot - no report as from a rifle
a bow would be better

we were shooting from the Packard at bottles

I drove, he shot
gallon bottles at 40 MPH he couldn't miss

& that night a man killed shot with a shotgun
the killer in a car fired on the move
we had nothing to do with it, wondered
had the killer practiced that afternoon

maybe he knew he would hit his mark

Chicago everybody came from Chicago

Nobody's Child

she turned me into an elf delighted jumping
the bell ringing ringing
some strong man bringing down the sledge
sending the weight

again & again to the bell

she's never been to a carnival

no conception at all

the old man smiled at our holding hands

If he's such a bore, why do you sleep with him?

*

were looking for a five-pointed star
found one with four, another with six
eucalyptus buttons, Golden Gate Park

the cape was red velvet
(what a big nose you have grandmother)

she rode into Stinson in a white Cadillac
angels fore & aft
hell's angels leading the way
the black & the white

there was an old stove in the hotel
we sat out back, sunshine & grass
lilies & orange california poppies

she made friends with the coyotes, the wolves
she never got to know
it was an experiment
she left before the results were in

we were seated in the big chair

the quilt is the same color as those poppies

This is not the way I'd have done it.

if you had to be interrupted –
do it in style, Sam making corn bread,
                                        Neal passing thru

the bottle fell, exploded
        pictures

watched squirrels, the park, Sacramento
hot coffee on her raincoat coming home, the city cold

the donut shot, or over Sutro Baths, New Lucca

(Big John's?
        – were you dancing there the night I was there?)

amusement park pictures
out the window, near the tunnel, broadway & Larkin
who found you???

                        there are horses tethered in the woods

                    *

an earring, broken, hanging from the light string
        near your bed – I could reach it from the bed

the Dansk candle holder

one of the two long towels, thin stripes of blue & red,
        green, yellow & black, hung as curtain, to keep
        the late morning sun from the bed

the dresser, the drawers empty, the mirror –
a nearly faded flower? painted to one side
in green & red

(I sat on the bed, watched you in the mirror
as you brushed your hair, your chin up
head back, then lowered – the final look
before you turned)

the ice cream maker, a half empty bag of salt

these were the last of your things

two boxes of your old clothes sit in a corner
the house filled with strange people

I TRIED TO WRITE YOU A SONG

    there was a swallow in May
    a hummingbird a fuchsia

it was an ancient song
with no beginning nor end
    like morning light
    medicine bells
      bee stings

    like broken glass & red beads

all the clocks were faces
  set at ten-twenty

>   out of the dark
>   stars stars configurations
>   fell in the gravel

Do you have your gun???

>   (he had to back all the way out
>   one-tenth mile down hill
>   drove home alone —
>
>   a messenger of the gods
>
>   no mercury, nor packard, but a chevy)

she arrived for her birthday

I filled myself with rye
(it was a very special midnight)
let her shine on me

we were both born that night

(I wore my work shoes)

naked but for swimming suits we stood feet together
your feet between mine in the sand
you looked up at me gray eyes one small fleck of gold
palms sway the breeze warm from the sea
our bodies warm dark from the sun
darker than our suits
in the darkness   there are stars over us   we kiss
up & down the beach figures move with the sea
on the shore a quiet splash of voices
it's all right you told me they can't see us

naked our bodies warm skin against skin
we made love in the grass your front yard
colored leaves orange & red yellow & brown
blow up around us
leaves burn in the street smoke over us
children talk playing laughing
it's all right you told me it's only a dream

SNOW ON MT. ST. HELENA

the mountain behind me, I drove south & west
passed three angels in Valley Ford
five more & a girl at the cross roads to Tomales
& four gassed up at Point Reyes Station, roared away
chrome & hair catching sunlight, to the north
to join the others

Billy & Toby were off, again
to Oregon, as per
I Ching, The Book of Changes

going thru changes

like music

harmoniously, minor discords
like she burned or threw away everything, always
burns her bridges
pulled the old light out of the ceiling
tore the wires loose, all connections

change gears

angels at every turn
all crossed roads

both sides, the streets lined with Harleys, choppers
of every description

> *he opened her coat*
> *& holding it open*
> *carefully & with expert eye*

examined
what she had to offer
so to speak, as it were

                              a whole world

& nothing ever dies, it's all here
on every road, behind every tree
growing out of the ground, a beautiful
fire, flames

                    I'm grinning

exhaust, carbon

                    diamonds & threads
my mind is filled with diamonds & threads

we go off in all directions,
                    thru intersections & crossed roads

a necklace to live in

SHE CAME TO GET ME — HER BIRTHDAY —
a 1938 silver Buick.
She wore the blue crepe gown, silver slippers.
I didn't ask where she'd been —
where we were going.
There was straw on the floor
blood on the back seat.
The toll collector smiled.

NIGHT STORM, THE MOUNTAIN, BRANCHES
in the road, winding & wet, driving
making time, I braked
again & again, as figures
stepped out, from behind trees
along the road, from behind mailboxes
stood, stepped out, into the road
men, women, & once
just off the ground, a blue fox

WE CHANGE TO KEEP ALL ELSE THE SAME

Crows fill the tree, get up
one by one, heavy, together
swing black across the blue
settle, one by one
together, fill the leafless tree

I burn six candles
white candles on a white plate

Six deer, dark in the snow, their heads
turned to me, & hawks
wheel above, blue sky
the deer do not move

Your hair has turned to Magpie feathers

CROSSED & CROSSED THE BARBED STEMS
but the roses brush, brush
come together
                    one rose, rolls in the wind
petals layered, honey & dew
rolling rose
            & the glow

I WAS CRAWLING AROUND ON THE FLOOR
with her sister, when she came in,
sat on the arm, the overstuffed chair
just so, her skirt adjusted, legs crossed
I have something for you, she said, held before her
two crystal balls, one clear, one ruby

VENUS, PINK, OVER THE TREES

                                        apple blossoms
            dropping off
            you dreamed I sent you away

I lighted the lamp, smeared oil
on your breasts your thighs your stomach

the branches fill, leaves & green apples

Jack Boyce circa 1970
© Zoe Brown

Bill Brown circa 1960
© Zoe Brown

Bill Brown and Jim Koller 1967
© Zoe Brown

Maggie Brown and Richard Brautigan circa 1966
© Zoe Brown

Richard Brautigan circa 1966
© Zoe Brown

Joanne Kyger circa 1970
© Zoe Brown

Philip Whalen circa 1967
© Zoe Brown

Peter Coyote circa 1970
© Zoe Brown

MARS, OPALESCENT ORANGE,
McIbbon's crystal ball reflects fire light
the sheen of ten brass shells whirring
she swings them over her very blond head

we dance as the moon disappears
howl & hoot dance drum
the orange moon disappears

she asks for a boy but I
bring none
she asks for a girl but I
only smile
                    she writhes on her back
comes & comes
                    hears us

we fuck in high oat grass
children in a circle around us

    "Here the world ends, here
  it begins. I fly between. Bring word
  after the beginning, before the end."

wide wings thru dark trees

all that he could catch of her was white light
        & the black behind

owl, just returned from the dead

      "I wasn't really there"

THE DEER, OUT OF THE TREES, DOWNHILL
the lake below, slowly, one foot
then another, down the dozed road

I had heard of her beauty

three hawks, low, crows below them
a calf, trying to stand
placenta still swinging from the cow

I caught her eyes

the owl, out of the trees
turns, returns
no place to come down

I CRAWLED OVER THE DARK GROUND
planting squash, an owl
over my shoulder, the moon

she throws back her head, stretches
her arms hands, ripple of muscle
skin, the moon

clouds, shadows
between us
the ground mostly lighted

the flower first, fruit
full & rounded
the softest curve, ripple, moon

the laughter very soft

"I get crazy in the full moon"

WE CAME OUT OF THAT CITY
like we meant to stay out
north across the bridge
thru Sausalito, & in Mill Valley
drank wine, ate Italian foods
Phoebe & MacAdams turned back
we went on, the truck's bed
filled, the canopy
rattling & slapping
we stopped for all
wanting to go with us

from Tamalpais
we took the ridge road
sunset golden hills
red sky & blue
the Pacific, back of Bolinas

there were deer at the bottom
grazing the south edge
of that meadow

LIGHTNING, COMING HOME
blue sky in the south
full moon moving
cloud to cloud, lakes lighted
dark hills behind the darker hills
passed a horned owl, ruffled
one foot on his prey, deer &
two coyotes running

harder & harder to leave, she said

apples fall, the rooster crows
gray foggy summer dawn
apples in heavy dust

they stopped going south, the city
their boy swung on the rope
we drank what booze there was
filled their car, apples & pears

IT WAS ALL IN THE STARS

He curled up with a wet dog
who kept moving – the two of them
went round & round

       for Bill Brown

All through the night they rode
circled the Pole Star

blue white yellow & red ribbons
an iron bell before me

next to the cedar stood an oak
– the road ran between them –
I hung a rope from the oak, climbed it
could see more of the mountain – gold – in the north

the goat Thunder – was killed at harvest
the dog ate her heart

we filled the room with hemp smoke –
owl claws & feathers
outside, I looked into the dog's eyes
saw a dead man under the cedar

the blond woman came down from the mountains
watched over the child's birth

drunk, I pulled on a string of blue beads & iron bells
rung them – the bottom bell came off in my hand
I walked ahead, the road muddy in heavy rain
she followed, baby bundled in her arms
the wind louder than the rain
where we came into the trees

where we'd watched for deer, along the river
the bell before me, a woman
crashed, killed herself
thrown from her car, her body under my truck

I found spotted mushrooms under the cedar

found a fox dead in the road – traded her skin
for the spotted feather of a golden eagle

with blue white yellow & red ribbons
I tied three sheep skulls high in the oak
at dusk with iron pots for drums
I sang a circle around the house & down the road

at midnight – the roar of a single motorcycle
then another & another – thirteen riders
beer to fill the bed of a truck
we sang, ran berserk, raced
all night over the dark hills – into & out of the flames
the best rider of them all fell into the coals
we pulled him out – unburned – put him to bed
he slept until dusk, was the last to leave

the child grew, one summer night squealed for joy
the iron pots rang where they hung
& the riders came again
burned their fire, all of the wood
in the morning one of them pierced the child's ears

when we left the place, he had returned
stood with others in the road, waved after us

rounding a curve, far to the east
a golden eagle flew up before us

THE WOMAN AT THE WAGON

Egil made dolls
stuffed the stomach of one with stones
broke the neck of another
They both worked

I told her of Egil
first time I met her
she was drying the dishes, or cooking
I remember the look in her eyes

He slept in the attic
I visited him there
I remember the dusty photographs
& the American flag

*

The dog woke her
barking in the darkness
It rushed about, attacking
the wings that filled the tent

She gathered twigs
set fire to them
Smoke filled the tent
Set things right

She climbed slowly
a fistful of hair
high into the cedar
She tied into the tree

*

Her eyes closed, & cold
I brought her back
Dreams of golden monkeys
I made sure she breathed

My back to the wall
I led her, over the roof, down
She would have a wagon
a horse of her own

There were other dreams
her unborn children
I heard her in the night
speaking to them

BEGIN WITH THE WOMEN SITTING —
their legs stretched before them in golden grass.
This is a place to begin. The women talk
softly in sunshine, of what we become.

We become more of what we have always been.
I stopped to comb my hair, my beard.
I stopped to get off. All those colors
through my temples. More of the same.

The winter shadow knocks down the fence row.
Where I am. Where I was. A sorceress
out of the blue. Her blue beads &
red tail feathers. Pale blue sky.

More of the same. I hear them moving their legs.
I hear the grass. The wind in those wings.
Twilight at the gate. Through the bay leaves.
Through the oaks & willows. The sky darkens.

& still more. They cook now, move
to their feet. There are fires on the skyline
& women moving. I lose their faces.
They have become shadows, between me & light.

I have lost sight of it all. The colors gone.
I have become more of the same. It is winter.
The hunting bird speaks darkness.
Speaks, speaks. Darkness.

Only a step away. But I cannot hear her words.
Only a step away & there is nothing.
I stop to get off. Comb my hair.
Begin where you are. Only a step away.

THE EAGLE WAS ON THE GROUND.
The Seri pulled his rifle
swung from his saddle, squatted & fired.
The sight was tied on with string.
He stood, grinning, watched
the eagle fly, up & out of range.

The women stood around the truck,
laughing to one another
brightly colored skirts, long black hair
pointing in at the small blond children.

I flew to the moon, he said, sitting in his corner
a skinned rattler in a clay bowl before him.
You heard that wind last night, that was me.
They'd been picking up wood, found the rattler
sunning himself.

We went to sleep looking at the stars,
the hunter & the bull
saw a comet when we woke before dawn.
I killed two scorpions in the morning.
They ran for cover as I rolled up the bedding.

The shelters were ocotillo, the spines burned off.
In winter they ate the yellow fruit of the cholla
slept under the white down of pelican skin blankets.

We chased a coyote with the truck
over the salt flat, to see him run.
We passed wolves hung dead beside the roads.

The spring in Libertad lies on the shoreline
below high tide.

GREASE CRACKLING, MY SOOT
black hands turning the meat,
passing the bottle.
We sat on our heels,
black hats watching the mountains smoke,
elk ribs on the coals.

SHE CAME NORTH LOOKING
for a truck, a chainsaw.
Bill was drunk & most of the night we sat at his table.
I climbed into my loft just before dawn, fell asleep
& she came looking for me, called
came up my ladder, lay with me.
We made a quick trip to the south for her goat.

Wild roses grew all around our small wooden house.
We planted a garden, watched it grow.
Our child was born.
Deer found the garden, tracks in the soft ground
& one day a buck, at dawn
stepped from the high wet grass

There is too much to say that can't be said.
There was too much to say that wasn't said.
I asked for a sign. It was given.

I fell, stood knee deep in snow
Santa Fe below me, the Jemez ridge
on the other side of the valley.
I came down to a trail
skied between close trees
until I came into the open.

LETTER

I didn't mean to take your Spirits from you
they fill me now & now
I know they are not mine
They will come back to you

Thunder showers in front of them
Thunder showers behind them
They will come back to you

I am sending back your Spirits

I have sent back your Spirits

SWEEP, SWEEP, BROOM
in his hands.
Gonna get it all together.

The stars ain't, I said,
together.
Took him out, showed him.

You gotta leave it
like it is, I said.

His women wanted
to go to bed.

WE'D COME FROM CALIFORNIA –
two days & a night, we were going home.
You sat beside me, wondering
where your mother was, wanting
milk from the jug we carried.
A long time for a two year old to sit still.
Flat tires, a bad carburetor. No way to hurry.
Second night we pulled off, went to sleep.
You curled in my lap, woke
at dawn, southern Colorado mining town –
hard hats with lunch pails, walking to work
their shoes in the gravel
beside our old white truck.

for Jessie

JACK SLEEPS BESIDE HIS STOVE, HIS WINDOW
his rifle in his hand, the bear
stealing his apples.

His words pass by me & in waves
wash around me.

All night, down –
California summer after dark rice & olive country.
There are still small towns.

Along the coast, the fog comes in.
The bar, thru the windows
I see myself, I'm there with Bill Brown.
We all wear black hats, walk
behind the yellow pickup.
Jack rides on the tailgate.
Waves his black hat.
We are walking to the cemetery at Red Wing,
up the dirt road.
I watch Eileen tie her cut hair into the top of a tree,
baby Ariel laughing below.

Nothing left but time to lose.

I spread my tablecloth
blue over her body, kiss her feet.
I look out from between her legs.
Where are your earrings?
I hold the back of her legs, her eyes
blink, hawk eyes.

The last bottle broken.
Blue clouds, thunder, lightning.
We are moving. I park the trailer

under the trees, in dust.
Water the dog.
Sam. Chief. Buck. Thomas.

Bring whiskey.
Dust lifting, miles & miles, the car
from above.

We're flying over the mountain,
down to the channel, the trees we planted.
I fly above the trees, the wires, come in
flap my arms, drop my feet, stand
between walk & old frame house.
I can't remember why I came down here.

I drive 100 mph in a green 1950 Pontiac convertible.
Jennie Smith, going the other way, stands
waves from another car.

You can't write everything down.

Several men with dogs
walk behind us. Time to go.

TAMALPAIS

He waded & swam the lagoon,
drunk & mad, walked most of a night
muddy & wet, to his tent
on the mountain.
His ashes blow there
with the bluejays
he chased from his camp –
his only newborn son, somewhere
there too, with him
on the mountain
where the old ones would never go
because the dead ones lived there.

for Jack

WE FIRED OUR RIFLES INTO THE DARKNESS
circled the flames, the snow
squeaking underfoot.
Towards morning the fire
burned down, a cold dawn.
Jays squawked, gliding
out from the trees, & back
with a snap of their wings.

Dear Lew,

I guess you know that Jack is gone.

Sitting here in my kitchen, drinking
another bottle of rye
I've been thinking about the two of you
all the times you drove out
from Cecilville & Forks of Salmon
a bottle between you

They'll never see you in Gazelle again.

Even driving through.

THE PATH TO HIS HOUSE
was lined with tombstones.
The house was all different.
Somebody else lived there.
In the dream Jack was alive,
on an island, his baby with him.
We're all right, he said.
Everything's the way it's supposed to be.
Get off the path, was Jack's advice.

American Beauty
Like a rose
in a book.

I had come out of the mountains to the east.
She told me, I had heard it before,
I'm going to have a baby.
Jack wore earphones, danced to the Dead,
Not even he
heard it all.

We are in a new land now.
All of us. There are no bright banners
no beads or ribbons or long hair
no old clothes. Everything is new.
We are in a new land. Everyone
speaks a new language. Moves
alone. Each & every single one
gone on.

Only the Dead
keep it alive.

The Spirits With Us Now

Excerpts from the Novel

I Went To See My True Love
(1988-89)

Why is it that, looking back, we think we can make
sense of situations and events which at the time seemed
to make no sense at all?

We don't see the past as it was. We look at it from
where we are. We look at it with the new information,
the new values we've accumulated in the time, now
itself past, between those situations and events and the
present.

Each time we watch a motion picture we see more
in it, or at least, we see different things. There can be a
saturation point, a point at which we know we've seen
what there is to see, but if we come back to it years later
we're often surprised. The motion picture memory
provides includes us and our capacity to view it is great,
almost without limit. That our perspective changes,
that we continue to change, gives us renewed interest in
the past, which we change as we include in it more than
was there.

Cleary has reviewed the same situations and events
for more than twenty years. Most who lived in those
times and places with him are dead, or no longer in
touch. They contribute no conflicting input. His
memory brings the sequence up a segment at a time.
Initially, the segments seemed to run at real time, but
then began to slow. Each time, seemingly, the scenes

were more elaborate, and he saw more in them. Now, what he watches seems in slow motion. The scenes have gotten longer because he notes minute detail. At the same time, each viewing leaves him with less sense of what each person actually felt. Their emotions are clearly there, he witnesses their emotions, but his own understanding is no longer emotional, is no longer one of quick recognition and response, rather one of extended rational consideration. He has assigned and reassigned seemingly appropriate emotions.

Cleary's mind has turned those situations and events from raw material to an almost finished product. The changes now will be small. The artist creates his piece by adding what was needed, removing the irrelevant. Had Cleary been able to view it earlier, he might have questioned his creation's present form, might have questioned why one thing and not another was included. Now he has no such problems. One's past is created as history is rewritten, appropriately, for the present.

———————

Thorbjorg was not her real name. She took the name from the sagas, a name either very appropriate for her, or one which brought with it an identity she chose to assume.

In the sagas Thorbjorg is described in some detail. She was one of nine sisters, all of whom could tell of the future, but the only one alive at the point she is described. She was invited to feasts by the curious, in the hopes that she could tell things of import that had yet to happen.

The ritual Thorbjorg enacted before her prophesy is also described, and worth note, because she brought it with her to California. She sat on a prepared cushion stuffed with chicken feathers. She wore a loose blue gown, necklaces of glass beads. She wore a hood, gloves, and shoes that were on the outside black fur, on the inside, white fur. She carried a bag made of the same furs, filled with who knows what. From her seat, she asked that certain songs be sung. In California, she asked, but the songs weren't known, and she played them on a jew's harp. When she finished with her songs, she said the following words:

Many spirits are with us now.
They are here
because our music
called them here.
The spirits wanted nothing to do with us.
The spirits had nothing to say to us,
but they have heard our call
and they have come.
Much that was hidden before,
hidden from me,
hidden from all of you,
is no longer hidden.
I see what was hidden.
We will all see it.

Her prophesy followed. She was good at it. What she told happened. Sometimes she wouldn't tell what she saw.

People came to think of Thorbjorg as more than a prophetess, attributed other powers to her. She was a big woman, with long and full reddish blond hair. She was beautiful, and so much the way she was that few men had the courage to approach her. The women who knew her best were in some way like her, replaced those lost sisters. These women often brought men with them, asked Thorbjorg to tell what she saw in the men; later they asked about the children they would have, ask that their children and homes be blessed, or cleansed.

When Thorbjorg first rented her isolated country house north of San Francisco it had been long empty. Boys from the area had gone there to drink, used it as a place to bring their girl friends. When they discovered the house had been rented, and they couldn't use it as they had, they trashed the place each time she left.

She put her powers to work. Two of the cars so badly collided as they hurriedly drove out the mile long rutted dirt road that they sat abandoned when she returned. That seemed to make things worse, provoked revenge, and she came home one evening to find her black cat dead and pinned with a hunting knife to her front door. When next her tormentors drove without lights into her yard, she awaited them, opened fire from the darkness on their cars, with a repeating twelve gauge shotgun.

If asked about her own past, Thorbjorg told little, would say, "I know more about the future." In the beginning, no one knew more than the fact that her flight to San Francisco had originated in Philadelphia; then later, that she left Philadelphia after undergoing treatment for an amphetamine habit which she tried to break by locking herself into a room.

For whatever reasons, when she arrived in San Francisco she sought out Richard Brautigan, who was then known to few who were not writers. When introducing her, Brautigan gleefully wrung his hands, described that first appearance. He had been drinking red wine and writing most of the night. Soon after dawn he heard an insistent knocking on his front door. He lay for some minutes, not certain he was awake, then not certain he would open the door. But he did get up, walked from his two rooms down the long hallway to the Geary Street front door in his nightshirt. As he walked he caught a chill, and when he opened the door he stood shaking, overwhelmed by the sight of her, not knowing what to say.

"I came to be with you," she said.

He said nothing, but turned, leaving the door open, and walked back to his bed. She came in, closed the door, and followed him. As he covered himself with his blankets, Thorbjorg removed her clothing. She carried little, wore all of her clothes, several cotton skirts, one over the other, several shirts and blouses. When she slipped into the bed, she wore nothing but long lapis earrings. The sight of her – he remarked on the mass of her red pubic hair – so excited him that he shivered all the more, and stopped only after she had wrapped her long arms and legs around him.

Thorbjorg stayed with Brautigan only a matter of weeks. He told that story too. He and she had gone with others by car to Marin, and returning, the driver noted that it was Sunday night and worried he would have great difficulty finding a place to park. Thorbjorg said nothing at the time, but as they neared their destination, she gave the driver directions, which he followed.

"There will be a parking spot at the end of this block," she said.

The driver protested that he saw none, but as he spoke, a car pulled from the curb.

Brautigan had been thrilled by the demonstration of her powers, and asked that she tell him then and there what his own future held. She refused. When he demanded to know why she would say nothing, she said, "Only know I won't be with you."

Laura was Cleary's daughter. Marie, her mother, preferred working to child care, and by the time Laura was five, her father had toilet-trained her, taught her to dress and arrange her things, to see things as he saw them.

In the afternoons after Laura's naps Cleary played his banjo and sang to her the songs he had learned as a child from his father, songs from the hills and plains of western Missouri. When Laura asked why the songs they sang didn't sound like the songs on the radio, Cleary explained that they were old songs, that they told the stories of real people who had lived long ago.

"Aren't the songs on the radio about real people?"

"Sure," Cleary said, "but they're about people who live now."

"We live now," Laura said. "Why do we sing about long ago?"

"We're singing about the people who came before us. We're here because they were here. They were our people. We do things the way we do them because they did them the way they did. We even think what we think because they thought what they thought."

When Cleary and Marie made plans to move from Washington to California, Laura asked, "Why don't we move back to Missouri? Grandpa and Grandma would like it. Me too."

"Once people tried to stay where they were born," Cleary said. "Now people have to go where they can work, or where they can make the most money, or live best on what they do make. That's why Grandpa's family moved to Missouri, why they left Kentucky, why they left Ireland in the first place. Your momma can make twice as much money in California as she can

94

here."

Cleary and Laura and the dog Loup made the trip to California without Marie, who stayed behind to work the summer on her masters degree. She would join them when her schooling was finished. Cleary was to find a two bedroom house within walking distance of the school Marie would teach in and the school Laura was to attend.

Cleary had known Bill Anderson in Missouri, had written him when plans to move to California were firm, asked if he and daughter Laura and dog Loup might stay a few days. Cleary hadn't seen Bill for years, learned little of where he had gotten to from the post-card giving directions to his place.

When Bill stepped out to meet them that first night as they pulled into his yard Cleary hardly recognized the little he could see of his bearded face. The place was in the hills, much reminded Cleary of similar places Bill had lived in Missouri. Bill lived alone, but his mother and father had driven out because his father was dying of cancer and had wanted to make one last trip to see his son.

Cleary had known Bill's father, was surprised to see how much he had aged. Cleary remembered the man from a time when he was no older than Bill now was, remembered him having the same wild look Bill now had. In his sickness Bill's father needed his wife's help to get to the chair where he sat and watched as Cleary and Laura spread their sleeping bags on the floor.

"I can see you're on the right track," the old man said, "getting the girl to sleep that way."

Laura didn't give Cleary a chance to respond. "I like sleeping on the floor," she said.

Bill followed Cleary to the new house on his chopper the day they moved in, helped empty the trailer. Away from his dying father Bill could think his own thoughts and talked as they worked. There were people he wanted Cleary to meet, things he had to see. Bill was anxious to share his life with someone who had come from the same place he had.

"I only work when I have to," Bill explained. "I do tree work then, with a man called Little John. He fells trees nobody else wants to touch, trees with wires in them, dead trees, trees too close to buildings. When he's got one even he don't like, he calls me. Says he likes my attitude."

Cleary remembered the attitude. Bill was crazy. He came from a long line of people who took things further than they needed to go. In Missouri, because he was so like the Bloody Bill Anderson who had ridden with Quantrell and who had taught Frank and Jesse James much of what they knew, they'd called him Bloody Bill.

Marie questioned the need for Cleary to go to work. They were making much more money now, and if he worked they would have to find someone to care for Laura when she came from school. Her questioning never went to what Cleary felt was the truth of the matter, that she was fearful any job he might take would lead him to new things.

Soon after Laura started in kindergarten Bill told Cleary that the landscaping company where Little John sometimes worked was hiring. Cleary got himself hired.

Little John was breaking up a cement patio with a sledge hammer the day Cleary began work. Cleary introduced himself to John. That and many mornings Little John wore dark glasses until noon, when his whole body seemed to loosen up. On this particular morning Cleary worked beside him, removing the broken concrete by hand, wheeling it away by wheelbarrow to a pickup, where he threw the broken pieces into the truck bed to be hauled away.

"I'm an artist," John said. "Usually I do tree work, landscape only if I really need the work. Tree work buys the time I need to paint. You can't get ahead landscaping."

John lived with a woman named Lil, who was also an artist. "We met in a laundromat," he said. "You can tell a lot about somebody by watching them do their wash."

When he learned that Cleary had a daughter, John was thrilled. The one thing in his life that he wanted and didn't have was a child.

John had met Bill on a construction site at Big Sur. They had both hired on as laborers, where they'd worked together carrying lumber and ninety pound bags of cement up the steep mile long trail from the highway to the house site.

"It was a religious experience," John smiled.

"You're serious," Cleary said.

"Sure, life is a religious experience."

John mentioned that he and his wife Lil often joined Bill and others at a place in the hills of western Marin on Sundays. "The house sits back a mile from the gate," John said. "Dirt road, muddy at times, always bad. Thorbjorg rented the place. Then a group of women from the city moved out – women without men. Before long local cowboys were hanging around, then longhairs, bikers. Seems like one of the few places everybody's welcome. Some of the bands come through, too, sometimes play, or just hang out. Gets wild at times. Most of the crew are into guns. I've been out there when thirty guns, everything from shotguns to automatic rifles, were blazing away. Other times it's like a retreat. Heavy mood changes, like the women who live there. Maybe it's the moon."

Marie's fellow teachers were quite interested in "the alternative society," but followed it at a distance, it seemed, from what they told of their own lives. Marie guessed immediately from Cleary's description and apparent enthusiasm that Thorbjorg's place was likely in the thick of it. She had never known anyone who used drugs, had never been drawn toward the "mind expansion" that so many others seemed to want. She saw Cleary's and her own distrust of drugs as a good thing. When you had to function, how you were going to function had to be predictable, and had to be compatible with how everyone else functioned.

Marie and Cleary had noted the publicized exploits of Ken Kesey and his Merry Pranksters. Marie could identify with some of the stance, as most of the Pranksters were obviously educated and held values similar to her own, but much of it she found excessive, too like the pranks of college kids. Their behavior pointed to no alternative she wanted. Certainly, for her, any drug fixation was excessive and went nowhere. Beyond excess, Marie felt, there had to be true alternatives to the society she and other intellectuals had rejected for some time. Without true alternatives, she reasoned, there was little to it beyond negative statement and wantonly destructive behavior which crippled the efforts and systems of even those few who tried to function effectively. Her classrooms made it clear. Her students mirrored any public behavior and she found herself having to defend an establishment she couldn't justify defending just to get across those things she knew the students would need to function.

Cleary spoke with Little John of Kesey as well. The

two agreed that Kesey had captured the imagination of huge numbers. He had become a folk hero, the outrageousness of his style mythic.

"You take your chances and you pay your dues," John said. "Kesey will pay his. But what a ride."

Only after Kesey's return from Mexico, when he opted for what even then seemed a personal rather than social good, did John and Cleary relate his behavior to group behavior. He made a choice that, once it was there for all to see, would be followed. His choice would effect changes far beyond the moment, would transform a milieu by affirming individual rather than group good.

"Certainly a man's life is his own," John said. "But what you do affects others. We're all part of a whole."

"No man is an island," Cleary quoted.

"A single body."

"The mind needs some work."

———————

Loup understood that his life was connected to the car that he and Laura and Cleary had driven south in. Anyone watching him knew that he knew the sound of that car, could hear it coming long before any human. If he were stretched out, asleep, he would lift his head, listen, then stand, stretch, pace, sometimes even dance, front feet down, then back feet down, in anticipation of its arrival.

When the car broke down and Cleary traded it in on a pickup Loup was quick to learn that the pickup meant at least as much to him as the car had. Because the pickup always ran it was used more, was integrated into the life, and Cleary's life was no longer still. There were places to go, people to see. If not on the seat with Laura and Cleary, Loup rode in the truck bed, stood with his nose into the wind, watching the world come at him over Cleary's left shoulder.

Loup was a big dog, could rest his jaw on the normal table without stretching his neck. Laura encouraged him. Marie thought his eyes "soulful." Cleary laughed with him.

Though Loup was solidly built, his chest and neck well-muscled, he was curious, and his curiosity gave him a busy look that enabled him to move, despite his size, without notice through most situations. Few watching him realized how totally aware he was of those things, people or animals that he moved through. He was not generally aggressive, but moved as Cleary himself moved, seemingly in his own indistractable direction.

Loup's first visit to Thorbjorg's began when he was attacked by two Great Danes, a German Shepherd and a Beagle. The dogs, who lived there, greeted each car or truck as it entered. Loup jumped from the truck's bed as Cleary opened his door. The Beagle grabbed a rear leg. Loup arched back and the Shepherd went for his throat. The dog mouthed little more than thick hair and loose skin, but once his jaw closed, he couldn't afford to let go. One of the Danes took hold of the top of Loup's skull, his teeth through one ear. The second Dane tried to grip Loup's spine, but found Loup's back too broad and hard. He tried again, further back, for the narrow between chest and hips.

Cleary responded even as Loup. He grabbed a two by four from the bed of the truck, beat off the second Dane and the Shepherd, but the first Dane held tight to the skull, the Beagle to the rear leg, each withstanding repeated blows. Cleary dropped the two by four, took the Beagle's rear legs and twisted the dog's body until the pain in its own jaw and neck forced open its teeth. Spinning, Cleary threw the dog as far as he could. Loup's skull was so broad the Dane was unable to close his mouth. Loup forced his head up, not allowing for a shift of grip. Both dogs knew when Cleary joined in that the standoff couldn't go on. The Dane's loss of attention, once he turned to Cleary, enabled Loup to twist free. The Dane's teeth tore through Loup's ear, ripped back his scalp.

Cleary grabbed up the two by four again, but before he could strike another blow, he realized the dog's owners were calling their dogs back.

Laura wrapped her arms around Loup's neck and Cleary examined his head and body, but the dog was anxious to explore. Cleary patted down the flap of loose skin, would watch it for infection.

Thorbjorg kept a small white dog, a long-haired female, which in its youth had suffered from distemper, and had as a result a twitch in the muscles of its one brown eye. The other eye was such a pale blue that many thought it white. From her size and general manner, many thought that she was partially coyote. Her eyes and this coyote nature made it seem that, like Thorbjorg, she knew more than she let be known. Thorbjorg called her Huginn, after Odin's raven. "A black name for a white dog," she once said, and added, "but it fits."

As Loup's first visit continued he became aware of Huginn, aware too that the Shepherd who had gone for his own throat followed her everywhere.

Loup sat beside a board fence, a fence along which two fair-sized logs lay. Huginn saw him sitting, and moved to greet him. As Loup stood, the Shepherd, perhaps carelessly assuming he had established his position, moved between the two. Loup slowly stood, and when the opportunity came Loup threw the weight of his chest and shoulders against the Shepherd, knocking it fully onto its back between the fence and the two logs. The Shepherd twisted, trying to gain its footing, but Loup was at its throat. Thorbjorg screamed a strange bird-like scream which she knew would demand Loup's attention and gave others the chance to come between the dogs.

———————

Cleary collected topographic maps of the counties immediately north of San Francisco and tacked them to the bedroom ceiling because they needed so large an area they would fit no wall. The route he drove to Thorbjorg's was one he laid out from the maps. As the pickup passed between the scattered frame buildings of one of the few small villages the route took him through, Cleary noted several bikers clowning beside their choppers on the edge of the road. They were waiting for something or someone. He recognized them when close enough as friends, men who rode with Bill. He waved to them, and they waved or nodded response.

Marie felt strongly that she was along only because she was Cleary's wife and he enjoyed the gatherings at Thorbjorg's. He so much as said that he wanted her and Laura to share the experience with him. Neither of her first two visits had been in any way exceptional. She had met and liked Little John and Lil, but none of the others had had much in common with her. She felt most were immature, pretended to be what they weren't. She had encountered no significant conversations, little beyond small talk, for the most part regarding things or people she knew nothing about. She didn't like the fact that so many openly used marihuana. She didn't think Laura should be exposed to it. Cleary wasn't worried about it. He felt greater harm came from its being illegal than from its own powers. Drugs had become a topic with her fellow teachers as well, and though no one openly admitted using them, their points of view could mean they did, but were afraid to jeopardize themselves by saying so. She herself, Marie realized, had avoided mention of Thorbjorg's, as though the place itself might bring her harm once she   were connected to it in the minds of others.

Laura stood on the truck seat between Cleary and her mother, looking at the road behind them. "It's Bill," Laura yelled.

In his mirror Cleary watched the choppers coming up fast. Bill, in the lead, slowed, settled in beside the truck, beside Cleary's open window. He tried to make himself heard over the engines. "You headed for Thorbjorg's?"

Cleary knew he'd never be heard, shook his head, "yes," grinning.

"See you there," Bill yelled, pulling ahead even as he spoke.

The other choppers passed, one by one on the narrow road. Cleary watched them pass. The moment had some movie reality – you could linger over the details. Like slow motion, he thought. They all looked like they were trying to be the bad guy in a Sergio Leone western. Cleary had never noticed how bad his friends looked. Maybe they were bad. He laughed to himself. Maybe we're the bad guys. He was sure Bill was the baddest.

A white Cadillac convertible followed the choppers. Cleary counted the five women in it, noted both their beauty and and their hardness.

"What do you think?" Marie asked.

Cleary turned to her, surprised, caught in the act. "One man's poison is another man's meat," he said.

"What does that mean?" Laura asked.

"Means you have to pay attention," Cleary said.

Marie's reservations about Bill were something she didn't feel she could talk about. He was, after all, a long time friend of Cleary's, had grown up with him, and though Cleary had gone off in his own direction, they had many things in common. Many things she didn't like in what she could see of Bill were things she didn't like about Cleary. It did in some way relate to their Scotch-Irishness, which seemed to give them both the ability to expect and create tensions where none existed, and then to attack with a singlemindedness that might easily destroy all concerned. They were both very alive, at their best, or worst, depending on your viewpoint, when in the midst of catastrophe. Cleary often grinned, but there was a special grin that he saved for moments of great intensity and activity.

Cleary came around a curve to find the procession stopped.

The girl had been hitching, and Bill slowed, passed her by, but then stopped beyond her, and when the others had come to a full stop the Cadillac was beside her. Cleary stopped behind the Cadillac, watched her get in, watched while the women made room for her to sit. She stood in the back, full face, before she turned, sat, as Bill and the procession rolled forward.

Cleary couldn't get that first sight of her out of his mind, even after the Cadillac had distanced itself and he could no longer make out the wild blowing mass of her dark hair.

Looking back, Cleary remembers well the loose fitting well-educated school girl look that characterized Ruby when he first saw her.

In reconstructing that day he starts by imagining her standing beside the road, the look on her face as Bill and the others came into view.

Her blue eyes were laughing, but there was an "Oh, oh, what do we have here!?" look. In the smile there must have been a touch of that determination that would carry her through it all.

"You look like a flower," Kesey had said. "Can we call you Ruby Rose, like some fairy princess?"

"Why not?" she laughed, blushing.

As Ruby later told it, Kesey then spotted his wife watching them and pulled from his pocket a long-carried packaged rubber, waved it so she might see it. Ruby said she didn't understand what the gesture meant, but didn't ask. That he was married, that his own thinking was so clear to her, was enough. She curtseyed, thanked him for her name, joined those fellow students from Stanford who had brought her to sit however briefly at the round table in La Honda.

———————

There were those who took their acid in quantity, went for the total personal experience. Others found that frequent small hits kept them on an edge which allowed for greater overall social functioning. Thorbjorg was one of the latter. She said what acid in such small doses did for her, much as wearing someone else's glasses, was to give her own view a dimensional warp it didn't otherwise have. Because she already saw what no one else saw, knew and told of things others didn't, such vision intensified, and at times she seemed to cross over, not leaving those with her, but moving among the unseen as well, interacting on levels beyond any that the others might see, except as those others could watch Thorbjorg herself.

Midway to the buildings the road dipped into and ran along a ravine before it climbed. Along the ravine there were trees and shrubs, many birds. Once above the ravine there was only pasture until the road reached the buildings, the trees and shrubs around the house itself. Thorbjorg said once that she considered that her place began with the ravine, that it rather than the gate established her perimeter. She had found, somewhere in the trees along the ravine, a spot, "where things were just right," she said. She told no one where the place was, wouldn't go there when she knew others were about.

Cleary watched for Thorbjorg, as he drove through the ravine. Cleary's grandmother had believed in the spirits, had spent hours sitting beside him as he lay sick, telling him of the spirits. He remembered thinking as he lay there that it must all be true, his grandmother didn't think she was making it up, really believed what she said, in fact, related much of what had happened to her to the sprits. He had wondered then why no one else had been affected by them, had reasoned that if you didn't know they were there, you wouldn't know the part they had taken. Or maybe if you didn't believe, they weren't there, or had no effect. You obviously didn't have to know about the spirits to get along in the world. There were so many other factors working on you, and it was so difficult to sort them out, that it was maybe best to leave well enough alone.

Cleary liked the view as he crested the last hill. He could see the house, the old frame farm house, trees around it, all oaks and willows, the toolshed, the barn, Thorbjorg's cabin. The parked cars and trucks were in clusters, like camps. Some were indeed camps, with house trucks at the center of them.

As he dropped toward the house, Cleary spotted a

woman in a long white dress up near Thorbjorg's cabin. She was alone and seemed to be dancing in the high green grass.

———————

Cleary guessed where Loup was headed, was right behind him when Loup found the hanging deer. It had been gutted but was not yet skinned. Cleary offered his services.

Loup knew that something would eventually come his way if he kept his eyes open, and hung back, circled the project several times, and lay, with his nose on his forepaws, watching.

Huginn alone greeted Loup, then with great delicacy she lay beside him, just ever so much closer than he to the hanging deer.

Those watching quickly realized Cleary knew what he was doing, and that he had the tool to do it. He cut only as needed, peeled back enough to hold onto, and holding it, used the heel of his other hand to force the skin free. As Cleary worked he circled the deer, took note not only of the deer but of those who stood near by, those who passed. He saw Thorbjorg, in the long white dress, moving alone, almost as if she were blind. Laura sat near Loup and Huginn, watched Cleary's work as intently as the dogs did. Cleary didn't see Marie, Lil or John. Or the girl.

Bill's voice came from near to the fire, with the voices of several others, the sounds of drinking. He joined Cleary when the deer skin was free, and he took up the hacksaw, sawed the deer's spine from neck to tail. Other bikers took to the deer halves with their knives, cut the meat as directed, Bill ready with the saw as needed. When the men moved to the fire with the meat they were bloodied above the elbows, their faces, where they'd wiped away sweat, smeared with blood.

Loup and Huginn moved in to clear the butchering site, kept the other dogs back with bared teeth and growls.

Cleary and Laura looked for Marie, found her drinking white wine from a stemmed glass, talking with Lil. Cleary sensed he was moving between realities, from the world of his own childhood, where the concern was survival, to a world of garden parties. The two women looked to be aware of little beyond themselves and their glasses.

Lil was doing all the talking. She seemed nervous, puffed at her cigarette, put it out, then fiddling with her lighter, still talking, lit another.

"I wanted to know what was going to happen to me," she said. "I wanted to know whatever I could about how my life would go, and when I discovered that Thorbjorg did such things, I asked her. She's really very direct but I couldn't get her to say anything at first and I kept after her. That she didn't say anything worried me. I was sure something really bad was going to happen. Finally she told me that I would live a long time, that I would suffer great sadness, but that I would get over it. I asked her why she hadn't told me right away, why she let me worry. She said she wanted to be sure she said it all in the right way. She apparently had to think about it."

Cleary wondered if he himself would someday ask Thorbjorg about his own life. In some way it was as simple as asking your mother what was for dinner, you were going to eat it whether you liked it or not. Maybe knowing could get you ready for it. Once again he thought that it was also possible that things could happen because you thought they were going to happen. You could bring things on just because you thought they were coming.

Cleary turned to look for a drink. Somebody near the fire strummed their guitar, and that seemed a likely direction. Laura started after him, then turned back. "I'll tell you when the meat is ready, Mom."

All the women from the Cadillac but the one Cleary hoped to see stood around the fire. He didn't know what there had been in that quick look he'd had, but he knew it had given him a taste of something he had to savor. He was being drawn to her almost as though she had him on a long line. Too long a line, he laughed to himself.

Ruby had heard of Thorbjorg from friends in San Francisco, had learned where she lived, had learned that on Sundays Thorbjorg was always there and that she very often had something of import to relate. Ruby wanted to see it happen, as she had wanted to meet Kesey. She wanted to be part of the dance itself, she thought.

Things weren't happening quickly enough. Ruby recognized that most of the people knew one another, saw that they quickly settled into familiarities. It was more like a large family gathering than a party, where everyone was eager to meet everyone else.

She had seen the woman in white on the hill as they drove in. She'd guessed the woman was Thorbjorg, and once separated from the girls she'd ridden with, she'd gone looking for her, but Thorbjorg was no longer near her cabin. Ruby peeked in, saw that it was draped with fabric, much of it tie-dyed. It looked, she thought, like the inside of some nomad's tent. But Thorbjorg wasn't there.

Ruby started back down the hill, picking spring

wildflowers from the grass as she walked. When she approached the barn, she turned to it. Entering through the large arch where doors had once hung, she heard large wings above her, and startled, turned half away before she turned back to see what she could in the dark space. She watched the owl fly from the far end of the building.

Leaving the barn, excited by the owl, Ruby almost walked into the large wolf-like dog that stood just out of the door. He seemed as surprised as she, seemed almost to smile sheepishly. When she laughed he came forward, greeted her by nudging her between her legs.

"Now, now!" she laughed. Right to the point, she thought. "And who might you be?" she asked, scratching his ears, careful to avoid the healing wounds she found there.

"We call him Loup," Laura said.

"I seem to be missing everything," Ruby said. "I didn't see you standing there."

"We saw you," Cleary said, "which is the important thing."

What does that mean? Laura instinctively thought, looking up at Cleary.

Cleary had seen Ruby from below, while she was still near Thorbjorg's cabin. He had tried to leave the fire alone, found not only Laura but Loup as well with him. But it worked just fine, he thought, remembering how often before strangers had talked when he walked with Laura and Loup.

"I was looking for Thorbjorg," Ruby smiled, aware that she was for some reason almost blushing. "I thought she'd be somebody to know," she laughed. "Do you want these flowers?" Ruby asked, offering the flowers she'd picked to Laura.

As Ruby and Cleary continued to talk Laura paid

attention. Cleary was not behaving in any fashion she was familiar with. She knew something was happening, but she didn't know what, and it made her feel strange. "I'm going to check on the meat," she said.

"Save some for me," Cleary said.

Laura ran down the hill. Loup watched, thinking to stay, then changed his mind when he saw where she was going.

Cleary sat down. Ruby didn't. She was sure that if she sat beside him he wouldn't get up. He was clearly a married man. She didn't want anything to do with married men.

As they continued to talk Ruby grew impatient with herself. Why didn't she just walk away? There was clearly something about the man she liked, even married, which frightened her.

Some minutes had passed when Cleary finally said, "We should go back to the fire."

Ruby thought, You should go back, but she didn't say it. She didn't want him to go. She sat down.

Little John's paintings were light and delicate, as the trees were to his eye, high in them, growing as they must, following patterns peculiar to their species, their own cellular structure. He was able to put into his paintings the simplicity of growth, lines that evolved, moved and became, mass that in its resolution transformed its perimeters almost without notice.

On the ground Little John had the sureness and easy manner of a cat, aware without attention. He preferred the trees, liked the distance they allowed.

"Once you understand," John said, "things get simple." High in the trees, John would concern himself with the direction some branch "wanted" to go. "I can make this branch go anywhere I want it to go, but first," he said, "I have to know where it wants to go."

John understood his own mind much as he understood trees. "When you're on the ground, you look up. In the trees, you look down. On the path, you look off. Off the path, you look for it. It all looks different, depending on where you are. But all you're trying to do is figure out how it wants to be."

Different drugs, because they do different things, gave John the possibility of looking at his mind as well as the world around him from different perspectives. He used the drugs he used when he was alone, or when that possibility was there, should he want it. He understood his relationship to drugs much as one might see his relationship to a teacher, a relationship that was to be respected, learned from.

Where better to pursue such studies than Thorbjorg's?

John had found his own special place in the ravine, a large oak he could climb, sit where he had a view of almost the entire ravine, the roads leading to it from either side. Lil alone knew when he slipped away what he was at, but even she didn't know where he went. He didn't always go to his tree, or at least climb and sit in it. Things had to be right.

Lil had told him of her question to Thorbjorg, and of Thorbjorg's response. When he saw her dancing in the grass near her cabin in her white dress, John decided it was time. He would ask about his own life. Another way, he thought, to understand, to know how it wants to go.

Thorbjorg had not been there when he looked for her. Not at the cabin, not amongst the others when he passed through them, though Lil said she had been there. He checked the buildings around the house and when he couldn't locate her, headed for the ravine.

When walking one must make noise, he thought, so as not to step on unsuspecting beings. Buddhist thoughts. He wanted Thorbjorg to know he was coming. He started to sing, a wordless, chant-like song. He was surprised by the sound of it, which reminded him of sounds he had heard once at a Navajo healing ceremony. He was surprised, because he was certain he had not learned what he sang, wondered at its presence.

What it wants to be, he thought, as he continued.

John did not know where Thorbjorg's place was. He knew that she had one, as he did, knew that he would find her, and when he saw her leaning against his own oak, knew that he needn't have worried that she didn't know he was coming. He made no greeting and Thorbjorg stood with her eyes closed.

"What was hidden is no longer hidden," she said.

There was nothing to say. Thorbjorg knew why he had come. John had the distinct feeling that someone had taken hold of his intestines, was about to remove them from his body.

Thorbjorg moved from the tree, stood, with her back to him. "I see a child," she said. "I see the child you have always wanted." Thorbjorg turned, her eyes on him. "He is dead. He is on a mountain. You are there with him. You are both dead."

The hands pulling him apart were cold.

Thorbjorg's mood was suddenly different. She half turned, stroked the inside of one of her long legs. "You'll live awhile yet."

John felt the sounds in his throat. It was the chant again.

Thorbjorg turned her back on him, ran her hands slowly from her waist over her hips, down her thighs. "He isn't mine," she said. She lifted the white dress, slipped it over her head, shook down her hair. "What was hidden, is no longer hidden."

John stood, unable to move. He watched Thorbjorg move, the lift and fall of her hips, the twist of her spine, as she walked from him, picked her way slowly from the ravine.

In time he stopped chanting. He hadn't moved, he realized. He was aware now that his mind was moving, he was watching it, had not been. He remembered the feelings, was aware of bringing them back. In some way Thorbjorg's revelation had driven from him that part of the mind that reflects, notes sensation. He had experienced his death. But it would be awhile yet, he thought. He was back. But he had been gone, he remembered the breeze moving through him, the sense, when he now reflected on it, that he had returned.

———————

Bill watched the meat cook, turned each piece several times to ensure that it didn't burn. He did it quickly with his bare hands. He was drinking tequila, and he felt no pain.

Laura had made friends with a girl her own age. As she passed with her new friend, Bill heard her say, pointing to the meat, "That used to be a deer."

The fire was very hot. All the wood had turned to coals, pale in the light.

"Am I the only motherfucker who can stand this heat?" Bill bellowed. He was by himself, all the others well back.

Thorbjorg was suddenly beside him. She hadn't put her dress on, no longer even carried it. "You're one of a kind, Bill," she said, and turned from him, to the fire.

"Jesus Christ," Bill said, taking her by the arm,

114

"put some clothes on, there's kids around." Saying it, he looked for something near him she might wear. He laughed. "Give me that skin," he said.

The woman who had taken the skin, stood, picked it up, needed both hands to throw it.

Thorbjorg stood still as Bill wrapped her in the bloody skin. When he stepped back to admire his work, she moved, as a deer, danced as a deer, lay finally as a deer beside the fire. "Take my body," she said.

One of the closest bikers responded. "Love to," he said.

Bill's voice boomed. "That means eat the meat." Even as he said it, he moved to the fire, threw a chunk of meat to the man who had spoken. He reached for another piece.

"Take my body," Thorbjorg said, quietly.

"Jesus Christ," Bill said. He put the meat in his mouth, bent forward and lifted Thorbjorg, carried her toward her cabin.

Cleary would always have that first picture of her in his mind, the way she moved and stood there before she sat, the wind in her hair. He didn't understand then, or ever, what it was about Ruby that so drew him, broke through into his life much as a large bird might fly through a window into one's home. It didn't make sense, would never make sense no matter how hard he tried to understand. She was there, suddenly, a reality that had to be considered, however out of place, however disruptive, beautiful and demanding attention.

Cleary had been married eight years, liked being married, loved his wife, loved his daughter, couldn't imagine another life, yet Ruby undeniably filled him with feelings and desires he knew threatened that life. One tries to unify one's life, to bring all those disparate circles together, to find in their overlapping space enough to function. But the bird in your living room is not compatible with any status quo.

When two flying objects collide, their tangential direction and respective speeds determine what course recovery takes. Having met Ruby would alter not only Cleary's but both their directions. Neither knew what to do with the situation.

Ruby, like Cleary, had relatively clear notions of expected behavior. A single woman didn't spend her time with a married man. If she did, she was asking for trouble. Either she was going to break up the man's family, or he was going to take her for a ride. Mother had explained it all often enough that it was well ingrained.

Ruby didn't want her mother's life, at least didn't want it at the price her mother seemed willing to pay. Ruby wanted a man who was right there, with her on all levels, mental and physical, a man who wanted to spend as much of his time as possible with her, not at his job, a man who respected her mind, a man who respected her body.

Cleary was very much where he was. Ruby knew instantly that she didn't fit any preconceived notion Cleary had about women. He was curious, interested, and willing to open himself to her in a way that was totally unguarded. He clearly wasn't out simply to get into her bed. He didn't have that manner. He wanted to know her. He wanted to share his life with her, wanted her to share her life with him.

What was important in life was the dance, and Cleary knew how to dance.

But what about his wife?

Ruby knew that she didn't want to destroy someone else's life. But maybe that wasn't what was going to happen, maybe Cleary and his wife didn't really belong together, were together out of habit.

Why was she being so silly? Cleary was just another human being. Just another person she liked, wanted to know better. There is nothing wrong with knowing someone. If there was to be more to it, she would deal with it when it developed.

When you are in love you are open to the world in a way you might not otherwise be. The sense you have of the world is not unlike the sense you have of the first day of spring, when you open the doors and the windows to let in the fresh air and sunlight.

Everyone who passes knows how you feel.

Marie saw the changes in Cleary. At first her own love went out to him, thinking that she herself had in some way rekindled the old feelings, but he couldn't reciprocate, wasn't there.

Cleary was embarrassed by his reactions. He did love Marie, but it was different. The image that came to his mind was the woodburning range that they'd had in Washington. There was comfort and warmth, a pattern of life that revolved there, a familiarity that once you had it allowed you to function in a very insular and unthinking way. You became annoyed when you had to pay too much attention, to focus where it was demanded, rather than where you chose to.

Marie was hurt, and in her hurt, pulled back. The evenings that she had so much looked forward to became times when she busied herself with class preparations and the general busy work of teaching. Laura and Cleary spent their evenings singing together, while she worked alone. She kept an ear open to the songs because she knew what they had always sung, and knew that if her suspicions were true, new songs, or a different flavor to the old, would emerge.

Marie was at first confused by the realization that certain songs she knew she had heard before she was now really hearing for the first time. They took on meanings she didn't remember. She discovered that refrains or pieces of the same refrain appeared in song after song. She thought it interesting to follow for herself the process of folk transformation, the slow flowering which created whole new songs from bits and pieces of the old. But she was listening to hear something more. She would find it.

The one phrase she settled on, heard in song after song, "my true love," was too obvious, she thought, yet there it was. Whether Cleary had sung exactly this or that song she didn't know. She did know he was singing it now.

Marie heard what she expected to hear.

Cleary thought later that Ruby's body was very much like his grandmother's, from some other time and place, in a way an archetypical body, one that would always demand male attention, regardless of the fashion of the day.

Ruby explained that she used no birth control. She feared the pill, which was still so new, and could not keep a diaphragm in place.

"And furthermore," she said, "I want a baby. I want a husband too." Ruby was smiling when she said it, but she meant it, wanted it out there again where Cleary had to take it into account.

He heard it, took it for what it was. He wanted to

ignore it, wanted to have Ruby as he wanted her, wanted Marie and Laura as well, and knew that no such possibility existed in Ruby's mind. He couldn't think of losing any of it. Maybe he could somehow keep it all together.

———————

Cleary compared people, their backgrounds and ideas and the way they lived their lives, everyone seemed to him a product of their past. However much you visibly lived a way other than you'd lived as a child, you were likely to respond in stress as you had responded as a child – in a pattern you were taught. In certain circumstances, if they were heavy enough, those patterns might be destroyed, but unless a new direction was right at hand, chances were that you would revert, pick up what pieces remained.

You could choose to be an outlaw because, though you put yourself on the opposite side, you working within the same assumptions, the same value systems you had before you made your choice. Even the outlaw, Cleary thought, acted more from learned patterns than from choice.

Certainly it wasn't all pattern, went further, to the nervous system. Some were born outlaws. Sometimes you ended up the way you did because you grew that way.

Thinking again of Ruby, Cleary tried to isolate what it was that drew them together. In her own way, which was admittedly quite different, Ruby was like his mother. Perhaps he was drawn to her for the same reasons his father had been drawn to his mother. She created a needed balance. That she was like his mother did not mean she had his mother's sense of it all, which sense he knew to be compatible with his father's, and

119

therefore, he assumed, his own. Cleary could only guess at Ruby's family sense.

Maybe it was all hormonal buzz, or maybe he had simply picked up on her attractions to him. No, he had felt it when he saw her at a distance.

At a distance. Cleary realized he had felt it without her input, without any actual connection to Ruby herself. It had originated in his mind. She filled some picture he carried within him, was at least in the beginning no more than a recreation of that image from his own earlier life. He knew her now, and there were things about her that fit, seemed to reinforce the image, but was he trying to discover what they were, or was he trying to fit her into the image?

He convinced himself that he was sorting out information.

Cleary didn't remember the exact point at which he learned Ruby was still seeing someone else. The information came to him slowly enough and with enough of his own understanding that he had not felt surprised but saddened. He realized that because he was married, and continued to participate in that marriage, Ruby too might need to continue a relationship, which like his own, had a history.

He was jealous, but felt trapped. There was nothing he could do to change things without first changing his own situation.

Ruby sat before her mirror, combed her hair. Cleary watched as she turned her head first one way then another, watched as she watched herself in the mirror.

"I'm to be in Stinson at six," Ruby said. She asked Cleary if he would drive her out. She would spend the night, would ride back to the city in the morning with Ben. It was his birthday and she had bought a bottle of the Russian vodka he preferred.

"We can go soon," she said, when Cleary agreed to take her.

It was too early, Cleary thought. "I suppose if we get out there too early we can stop somewhere – or do you want to get there early?"

"If we go soon we'll miss the traffic." She turned to look at Cleary, said, "I don't want to be late."

It was so obvious that Cleary laughed. "You're turning the knife," he said.

"You deserve it," she said.

"Because I'm married?"

"Because you want to stay married." Ruby turned back to the mirror. It was time for her makeup.

Cleary watched as she put on lipstick. She didn't usually wear it. He knew little about Ben. He and Ruby had both been part of the group surrounding Paul Butterfield's early days in Chicago. Ben was with the group one night in a Chicago bar called Big Al's when Ruby had come to listen to the Blues Band. She attracted his attention when she danced on the very small dance floor with the girl she'd come with.

"When did Ben come west?" Cleary asked, realizing for the first time he might have come with Ruby.

"We came together. We rented a place near Kezar Stadium together. It was horrible. We fought all the time. Ben had just returned from Mexico when we came west, had gone down there to trade guns for grass, and when he came back wanted out of it, but you can't leave those things behind. He couldn't."

Cleary came to know Chicago while courting Marie, whose family lived in a quiet residential area west of the city itself. He had heard much of the city's history, but knew little first hand. Ruby's family had lived on the fashionable north shore, in a house he could only imagine, having seen such places only when driving through with Marie, sight-seeing, looking at places Marie had once imagined she might herself like to live. There had been a wall, a gatehouse, a small house where Ruby's father's chauffeur had lived.

Ruby stood, struck a pose before the mirror. "I need a flower in my hair," she said.

Cleary said nothing.

They were early enough leaving the city that the traffic was light. Cleary turned off the highway at Tamalpais Junction, Route One, then turned onto the mountain road which hit Route One again just south of Stinson Beach. He preferred the mountain road to the coast road, liked better turning and twisting through the trees, the then sudden long view of the coast that you had only from so far above.

"I don't want to go up there early," Ruby said. "The place is small, and either Ben won't be there, or he'll be with someone else."

Cleary parked the pickup along the road at the edge of Stinson. Ruby and he got out, walked to a large and noticeably empty building above the highway. The building had surely once been a hotel.

The door was unlocked, and Cleary opened it. Ruby walked in. Cleary left the door open behind them. At what had been the front desk, Ruby announced, "We have reservations for the bridal suite."

In what Cleary thought an appropriate voice, he responded, "Those rooms are occupied."

Ruby turned, blushing, gave him the finger.

Cleary couldn't believe he was actually delivering Ruby to someone else.

She read his mind. "You're terrible to do this for me."

"Don't remind me," he said.

The hill below the hotel was covered with orange California poppies and tall green grass. After looking through the hotel, they sat in the grass, the highway and the truck below them.

At five Ruby announced it was time.

"The vodka is in the truck," Cleary said.

They held hands walking down through the high grass, kissed beside the truck, before Ruby turned, walked up the road. Cleary still sat watching her when she turned, midway up the hill, waved. Glancing in the mirror, he discovered there was lipstick on his face.

Ruby later told Cleary that Ben had not returned that evening, that she had waited all through the night for him, and then in anger, before she hitched back into the city, had torn his bedding from the bed, threw it and all his clothes on the floor, had poured the bottle of vodka over it all.

———————

The Donut Shop was across the street from Kezar Stadium, a place Ruby had gotten to know when she lived in the neighborhood with Ben. She liked the jukebox, which had more soul music than any other around. The two facing counters and display cases were in the front of the store, the jukebox in the middle of a wall lined with booths. Her favorite place to sit was in one of the few booths behind the jukebox, where she could keep an eye on it.

She had taken Cleary to the place soon after they'd started seeing one another, and it had become his favorite. The area was changing, in keeping with the times. Haight Street was turning from a residential shopping district into a street lined with shops and restaurants that catered to the hip crowd, to the tourists who came in buses to safely watch what was going on. The Donut Shop was around the corner, off the street. The people who came there were, in Ruby's words, "real people."

Cleary watched as Ruby put her quarters into the machine. Though it was nearly summer the San Francisco nights were cool and she wore her gray wool cloak, with its green trim. She didn't have the bounce she usually had as she slipped the coins in. The heaviness of their talk brought with it a determined set to her mouth.

"I don't want to be part of this," Ruby said. "I'm going to take a trip."

"Where will you go?"

She really had no plans, but she would make them. "I'll go visit my sister in Italy. Florence."

"How long will you be gone?"

"How long will it take you to make up your mind?"

"I don't know," Cleary said.

"I'll give you the summer. If you haven't decided something by then you never will." Ruby wished it was already decided.

A group of bikers came in, sat at the counter. Cleary thought the largest looked familiar. He couldn't remember his name, but Cleary was sure he'd been with Bill to Thorbjorg's.

"I don't know where I'll go if I leave Marie," Cleary said.

"You'll want to stay close to Laura."

"I meant I didn't know where I'd live," Cleary said.

"I'll find you," Ruby said.

The big biker turned on his stool in such a way

that Cleary saw part of a weapon holstered under his arm.

"Do you want me to go?" Ruby asked.

Cleary didn't want Ruby to go, didn't want to leave Marie, wanted everything to stay as it was, but it wouldn't, couldn't any longer. As Little John had said, it was time for Cleary to live alone.

"Maybe it's the best thing," Cleary said. "It gives me time to do what I have to do, and I won't be doing anything I'm forced to do." Except make a decision, Cleary thought.

Ruby already doubted her decision. He was right, he would make his choices on his own, but what if they were the wrong ones? "If you love me like you say you do, your choice should be an easy one," she said. She knew it wasn't. Laura was part of it, however much Cleary might not want to believe it.

Three Blacks came in, moved to the side of the counter opposite the bikers. Only one of them even noticed the bikers. Cleary caught a look between the big biker and the man next to him at the counter.

Ruby saw the change in Cleary's face. "What is it?"

"There's going to be trouble."

Ruby stood. "Let's go."

They would have time to get out, Cleary thought. Just time. He took Ruby's hand, walked to the counter. As he lay their bill and change on the counter, the big biker, who he suddenly remembered to be Big Mike, said, "Going to be a hot time in the old town tonight."

Cleary nodded, and he and Ruby were out the door. They walked quickly toward Haight Street. Cleary wanted to get around a corner.

"What did he mean?" Ruby asked.

"He was telling me it was a good time to leave."

In the Donut Shop Big Mike stood, grinning. The

other three men with him stood, all facing the Blacks who sat at the counter opposite them.

"What are you niggers doing in here?" Big Mike demanded.

The three men were drinking coffee, talking among themselves. One of them asked the man beside him, "Did you hear some jive-ass motherfucker say something?"

The counterman was quick to tell them to take it outside.

Big Mike laughed, spoke again. "*This* jive-ass motherfucker *did* say something. I wanted to know what you shit-faces were doing in here. You don't belong."

The three men stood slowly, moved slowly. "Those white girls over there," the same who had spoken earlier said, "sound like they need some big black cock. But they smell so bad."

No more was said.

When he saw that the Blacks would reach the door first, Big Mike slowed, pulled his pistol, but let the three men get out the door.

The gunfire started as the bikers reached the pavement.

The few customers left in the Donut Shop took cover where they could. The counterman was well below the counter. He tried to count the shots, but there were too many, fired too quickly. He stayed hidden until the gunfire stopped and he heard the choppers start, the wild laugh of the big biker as he rode off.

Marie was awake. She'd been drinking whiskey slowly since early in the evening. She heard a truck door close, and when she heard Loup moving under his tree, knew Cleary had returned. She set the glass on the floor beside the bed, beside the bottle, pulled the light blankets up around her head, turned away from the door. She didn't want Cleary to know she was awake, didn't want him to know she'd been drinking and crying all these hours.

Cleary entered the house as quietly as he could, didn't turn on any of the lights. He glanced in at Laura, looked quickly around. Everything seemed as it should be. He passed through the house, to the backyard, would pee in the yard, didn't want to flush the toilet. Loup was glad to see Cleary, pressed his large head between Cleary's hand and leg.

Back in the house Cleary decided to have a shot of whiskey before he went to sleep. When he opened the cabinet he saw that the bottle wasn't there.

Marie's voice reached him from the bedroom. "Bring a glass."

He did. Marie turned on her small reading lamp as Cleary came into the room. She was sitting up, the bottle in one hand, her own glass half-filled in the other. Cleary put down his glass, took off his boots and pants, picked up the glass, sat down on his side of the bed.

"Can I pour you a drink?" Marie asked.

"Sure," Cleary said, holding out his glass. He watched her pour the whiskey.

"Say when."

"When." The tumbler was half-full.

Cleary was sure Marie knew none of the details of his and Ruby's romance, saw no way that she could know. But she did seem to know there was a romance. He hoped she knew enough, wouldn't want any of the details.

127

Marie rubbed her swollen and red eyes. She started to cry. "I can't stop crying," she said. She was almost laughing as the tears ran down her cheeks. "I can't take anymore. I can't think about anything else."

"I don't want to lose you and Laura," Cleary said.

"It's too late now to worry about that. I don't know who you've been seeing, but I know you've been seeing someone. It can't just stop, and I can't take anymore. I can't live the way we've been living."

Cleary's conversations with John came into his mind. He knew Marie, once she had made up her mind, would be set in her decision – whatever might happen. If he could convince her that there was an acceptable middle ground she might stop short of a total breakup.

"Maybe if we live apart, but see one another often we can keep it from going too far," Cleary said. "I don't want to break up, don't want a life that doesn't include you and Laura."

Marie had not considered a middle ground. When she heard Cleary suggest it, she knew it would be better for Laura. Her own feelings probably wouldn't change, she thought. How could they, knowing that Cleary was out there somewhere running around with a woman probably much younger than she was – probably the girl she'd seen him with at Thorbjorg's. For Laura it would be worth a try.

The park was further from the apartment Marie had rented than it had been from the house. Laura would have to learn the way, Cleary thought, and as they walked, he pointed out to her the buildings and trees, landmarks, that he thought she would remember.

Cleary had been awake early, found that Marie and

128

Laura were still in bed when he arrived. After Laura had eaten her breakfast, Marie had suggested that Laura walk with Cleary to the park. Cleary said they would all go together, but Marie said she would rather work at getting her new place in the order she wanted it before she had to begin another week at school..

"Why is all this happening?" Laura asked. "Why are Mom and I living by ourselves?"

"This tree is a Deodar Cedar," Cleary said. "It comes from Australia." The tree was unusual, and Cleary felt Laura should note it. "I heard your questions. I'll answer them. But look at this tree."

"It almost has a blue look."

"The new growth at the ends of the branches is greener than the rest," Cleary said. "As the tree gets dryer it will get even bluer. Your mom and I decided that it was better to live apart than to live together because we were afraid that if we kept living in the same house we'd get so unhappy that we'd get a divorce."

Laura said she knew from kids at school what a divorce was. "Are you unhappy, or just Mom?"

"Remember that woman we saw up near the barn at Thorbjorg's?"

Laura stopped, looked up at Cleary. There was a look in those blue eyes he had never seen.

"Her name is Ruby," Cleary said. "We got to be friends that day."

"Do you like her more than Mom?"

"Nope. But your mom thinks I do. And it makes her unhappy."

"Did you tell Mom that you liked her best?"

"Sure, I did," Cleary said. He started walking again. "But that doesn't seem to have helped."

"Does Ruby want to live with you?" Laura asked,

catching up.

"She does," Cleary said, "but if I lived with her I couldn't live with you and your mom."

"Maybe if you lived with Ruby, Mom would let me come live there too."

"I don't think so," Cleary said. "If you weren't with her, your mom would be very lonely."

"I don't care who you live with," Laura said. "Just as long as you come to see me lots."

"I'll do that," Cleary said.

———————

Cleary sat at the old wooden table he'd bought for the house he'd rented in Sebastopol. The only light on in the house was the one in the ceiling overhead. He'd taken to writing down things that had happened, things he wanted to be sure he passed on to Laura. He looked at the blackboard leaned against the wall in front of him, the picture Laura had drawn of the house, the flowers in front of the house.

They had good times in the house. Somehow when he stopped in at Marie's, he didn't get enough of Laura, seemed to spend the time with Marie.

Laura kept a pile of clothes in Sebastopol to wear while she was there. Cleary had washed them with his own clothes on his way north. As he folded them and put them away, it was almost as though she were there too.

The house sat on a hill, some distance up a long gravel driveway from the road. There were no trees, and the sound of the car carried over the field between the road and the house. It had slowed as it approached the drive.

No one came to visit Cleary except Laura. He turned out the light, peered through the window as the dim headlights turned into the drive.

Cleary stepped quickly across the room, out the screen door, stood in the shadow of the house, where the headlights wouldn't hit him, and where he could see whoever it was get out of the car. It was Loup's favorite place to sleep, and the dog stood, watched and waited with Cleary.

He knew from the lights that the car was an old one. He hadn't seen many like it since the late 40's in Missouri. It was big, light in color. It stopped behind his truck. Its lights off, he could see that it was a 1938 Buick. It looked silver. When she opened the door, the dim overhead light silhouetted Ruby. A white lamb that had been riding on the front seat beside her tried to get out, but she held it back as she closed the door.

There was a laugh in her voice as she addressed the darkness. "Do you have a gun?" she called.

Loup was at her side, tail wagging, when Cleary reached her.

"How the hell did you find me?"

Ruby laughed. "I had to find you, it's my birthday."

Cleary couldn't understand how she'd found him, stood looking at her, trying to put it together.

Still laughing, Ruby asked if he didn't have a kiss for her. "I wore my party shoes," she said.

As Cleary opened his arms Ruby threw her arms over his shoulders and around his neck. It was a long kiss and Loup grew impatient, as a child might, came between them. He thrust his nose into Ruby's skirt.

She giggled. "Don't be rude," she said, and scratched his head with one hand while she held it, under the jaw, with her other.

"I guess he knows what he's looking for," Cleary said, grinning.

131

With her deepest voice, Ruby answered, "Me too."

They both laughed, and Cleary turned to the house, asked again, as he opened the screen door, how she'd found him. He had not wanted to be found.

———————

Once Ruby moved into her place in the Mission, she preferred that when she and Cleary were together, that they spend their time in the apartment. She had tried to interest Cleary into going with her to Cost Plus to buy furniture. She wanted him to pick things that he liked to furnish the place. He refused.

"It's your place," he said. "You know what you like."

She had chosen two bean bag chairs that took the shape of whoever sat in them, and then had stopped, bought no more than the necessary mattress. Her old dresser reappeared. She set up the two front rooms, the living room and dining room, as closely as possible to the way her previous rooms on Duboce had been set up. The only real difference was the red phone – she'd had a black phone on Duboce.

"The place is too big without you," she told Cleary.

The empty rooms reminded Cleary each time he passed them on the way to the toilet that he was expected to move in. It wasn't a feeling of guilt, he assured himself, but just an expectation wrongly held that he chose not to meet.

When he thought about how little food Ruby kept in the kitchen, how little he ever saw her eat, Cleary began to sense, knowing what he did about their life, that Ruby had become very unhappy. She wanted something she couldn't have, and was interested, so far as he could see, in nothing else.

Cleary asked her what she did with her days, told her he could see no signs of any life beyond the place. Ruby said she spent her time listening to music, drawing, or writing letters, or on the phone. "I still have a few friends out there," she said.

When he told her he was worried about her, she laughed, said, "Move in."

"Though I'm not living with my wife, we are still married. Not divorced. If I move in with you, it's exactly the same situation I was in before, except that you and Marie are in reversed roles. I don't want to do it. Living alone I can go where I have to, without apologies. Or lies. I'll keep my house."

Ruby screamed. "I thought you knew what you wanted!"

"I do know," Cleary said, not lifting his voice.

"So what is it?" she demanded.

"I just told you."

Cleary spoke to John about it all. John suggested that Cleary bring Ruby by to meet him and Lil. They were having a going-away party for a friend who was leaving for Japan. "Bring her then and she won't get the feeling we're analyzing her."

The party was too big for the small house and spilled out into a back yard that John had landscaped with shrubs Cleary remembered from their previous locations in Marin.

John had met them at the door. He wore his party clothes, looked to Cleary like an Irish bartender, with sleeve garter and the derby. He seemed to have been drinking for awhile, and his manner, as well as his clothes, made Cleary think of the "little people."

Cleary knew John well enough to know immediately that he very much liked what he saw in Ruby.

"Good to see that you could make it," John said. He laughed. "And this must be the girl I've heard so much about." He even said it like an Irish bartender might.

Ruby blushed. She had heard a lot about John too, and there was no missing how carefully he was looking her over. "I've heard a lot about you, too," she said.

Cleary recognized immediately that the meeting was beyond the ordinary. Ruby and John both liked what they saw, seemed to connect on a level beyond the moment. It was as if they had been destined to meet and were walking through parts they already knew.

Cleary threw his arms around them, drew both of them to him. They appeared to understand and share the feelings, and the three of them stood hugging one another when Lil approached, glass in hand.

Lil looked like something out of the 20's. She was wearing a short black silk dress with spaghetti straps that made her appear thinner and taller than she was. Cleary wanted suddenly to include her in the moment too, pulled her toward him.

Lil knew she'd had too much to drink and too much to smoke to do well with the situation. She felt she had to take it elsewhere. She liked Cleary, knew she was physically attracted to him, but knew too that he had brought Ruby, a woman she didn't know, and who seemed overly excited by meeting John.

Lil's manner more than suggested her priorities, made clear to all how it was that she wanted things to go. "Come meet everyone," she said, taking Ruby's hand. Ruby smiled back at Cleary and John, over her shoulder, as Lil led her into the room.

Lil stayed with Ruby, moved her from person to person, introduced her, initiated conversations which she then ended when ready to go on.

John had prepared a place of honor for Philip

Whalen, a throne, which Whalen was sitting in when Cleary and Ruby arrived, allowing his admirers and friends to bring him one delicacy after another. With his red beard and portly belly, the poet reminded Cleary of Santa Claus, except that his humor was dry and sophisticated. Cleary laughed to himself, Maybe there was more to Santa Claus than anyone suspected.

When there was no more, anywhere, to drink, the guest of honor let it be known in a wide variety of voices and antics. Lil, horrified, was immediately at John's side. He must leave that moment to buy more. How had he let it happen? "Be sure to buy enough this time!" she scolded.

Cleary caught up with John as he headed for the street. Ruby saw them, obviously on their way somewhere, and free from Lil, joined them. "You're not leaving me behind," she said.

When they reached the street, Ruby, who was holding Cleary's hand, took John's, and began to skip, pulling both men with her, until they too began to skip. The three of them skipped and laughed down the street and around the corner to the liquor store.

Cleary realized as he found himself driving up the dirt road that he had never been to Thorbjorg's on a Friday night. He had no idea of what he might find.

No one was there but Thorbjorg, who he found in the kitchen of the big house.

She was preparing vegetables given to her in the city. Cleary sat down at the long table to watch her work, and talk. She was wearing a loose and long shirt, and he watched her for some time before seeing that she was pregnant.

"No one knows who the father is," she said when

he asked.

Cleary laughed. "You mean you're not telling."

"No. I mean I really don't know." She explained that she had wanted a child, didn't want a man, and had made love to several during the time she'd conceived. She was sure the child would be a boy, a Sagittarian.

Cleary asked if she had picked a name, and she said she would wait until it was born.

"I'll know then what to call him," she said.

She suggested Cleary stay to eat some of the soup, and they sat for hours at the table, talking, drinking first tea, then coffee and finally the ends of several bottles that had been left behind.

Thorbjorg said she wanted to read the Tarot for Cleary.

"Why not?" he said.

She gave him the cards to shuffle, said nothing while spreading and picking up the cards, said nothing until she had closed the deck, placed it on the table between them.

"You are the survivor," she said. "The time ahead now is one of extremes, great good fortune, and death. Much will touch you, but you will be there to know the time is past. I see myself in your cards. You and I will see more of one another in the times ahead."

On his way to the truck, Cleary reached for a string of iron bells that hung on the porch, thinking to ring them. The bottom bell came off in his hand. He tried to tie it back, but the string was broken. He put the bell into his pocket. He would come back, could tie it on then, he told himself.

Cleary and Loup had started south soon after

Cleary had had his morning coffee. He had taken the bell from his pocket, put it before him on the dashboard, so as not to forget it.

He was on a stretch of road that curved through a small valley beside a creek. The road rose and fell with the curves and you couldn't see what was coming most of the time. The rainy season had just begun and it wasn't raining steadily, but the pavement, especially the blacktop, with its oils, was slipperier than one might expect.

The Volkswagen came around the curve and over the rise sideways. It was in the middle of the road, on a trajectory that would move it only very slowly out of Cleary's path. There was nowhere for Cleary to go. He hit the brakes. Loup slid off the seat. Glancing quickly, Cleary saw that on his own side of the road a hill climbed abruptly from the road's drainage ditch. On the other side there was a sharp drop. He held tightly to the wheel as he saw the crash coming. The truck was very nearly stopped when the Volkswagen's rear wheels, drifting toward the road's edge, hit the gravel, caught, and threw the car over the line, head on into the truck's left front fender.

Cleary knew Thorbjorg had known what was to happen. He had gone to see her because she wanted to see him, wanted to warn him. And the bell? Had the bell served to protect him? He took it from his pocket. He would take it back to her, would ask her. When the truck was ready.

He thought about Thorbjorg's prediction. He had always been a survivor. How would knowing what he knew now change things? It wouldn't. Or perhaps later it might make it easier to accept what did happen. But

137

he already knew that what happened was supposed to happen.

Cleary drove to Thorbjorg's directly from Santa Rosa after hitching there to pick up the truck. He didn't need to tell her of the wreck, the news had reached her.

He told her of pulling the bell from its string, being unable to tie it back in its place, how he had taken it home thinking to return it.

Thorbjorg asked if he had it with him when the Volkswagen had crashed into the truck.

He said he had.

"Keep it," she said. "Maybe it brought you good luck."

"You hung the bells there?"

"Yes," Thorbjorg said. She smiled. She knew he knew why the bells were there.

"I put some things together for the baby," he said. He handed her a small deerskin bag he had made, and filled, with things he'd felt seemed appropriate. "Maybe it'll be of use."

Thorbjorg took the bag. She was still smiling. She knew she didn't need to open the bag.

When Cleary left he was on his way to the city. He would spend the night with Ruby, had made plans to pick up Laura the next day, on his way home. He drove through Olema, turned up the gravel road at the Bolinas turn off. He wanted to drive the ridge road.

Climbing to the ridge, Thorbjorg returned to his mind. He saw her sitting as she had been when he left, in a loose long white dressing gown, her hair piled on top of her head. She was in a rocking chair, knitting. He hadn't asked when the baby was due.

The long view of the Pacific behind Bolinas made him think still again of Sergio Leone's films. He imagined the truck as seen from above, driving along the ridge. The truck wouldn't be moving, only the hills as he passed. He was on the edge of the world, with the Pacific out there. A harmonica played "Jesse James."

Cleary turned south beyond the Muir Woods turnoff, had crossed the first open hills, had dropped down into the trees, rounded the sharp curves that ended with the stop sign at Route One. Bill, on his chopper, turned up the road. He braked when he saw Cleary. They stopped side to side, only a short way above the stop sign. Bill parked in the middle of his lane.

"I read about your wreck," Bill said, standing between the chopper and the truck. "I don't know why I read it. I might have wondered if I knew the woman – said she died on the way to the hospital."

"I didn't know," Cleary said.

There were cars waiting behind both Cleary and Bill. Someone blew their horn.

"You OK?" Bill asked.

"Wasn't scratched," Cleary said.

"Didn't hurt the truck much," Bill said, glancing over it.

"Smashed the fender," Cleary said, pointing.

Bill examined it. "Did a good job fixing it."

Several cars were blowing their horns. Traffic was backed up into Route One, up the curve behind Cleary. Bill laughed and gave them all the finger.

Both sides of the street in front of the hall were lined with chopped Harleys parked rear wheels to curb. Most of the riders were inside, only a comparative few still with their machines. "The watch," Cleary thought. He heard music coming from the hall as he slowly drove past.

He spotted a parking place in the next block, drove past it, made a "u" turn, and parked. He had noticed as he approached the hall that police cars circled the area a block from the hall. One passed at the corner as he closed the truck door. They didn't want to get too close, he thought, just close enough that you knew they were there.

The music was very loud and most were on the dance floor when Ruby and Cleary entered the hall. There were hundreds dancing beneath the flashing and swirling lights. Ruby was quick to pick up on the excitement, the beat. "It's good," she said, "but it isn't Butterfield." She laughed, feeling the music even before they reached the dance floor.

Cleary had never considered himself a dancer. He had avoided high school dances, felt constricted by the regularity of the steps. He had learned the two step, made it do for all occasions. He and Marie danced only when they first met, and later, after they'd come to California, once Cleary had seen how dancing had changed. That you could move as you wanted to, that you responded to your partner's moves, rather than followed them, inspired him to try again, and once into it, especially when he'd loosened up with a few drinks, was able to free his mind of all else.

He was never able to stop when the music stopped. He liked best pieces like those the Grateful Dead did, long or bridged to others, that kept him moving as he wanted to move. Once in motion, he wanted to stay in motion. "Things in motion come to rest slowly," the I Ching said.

Cleary followed Ruby from the dancefloor into the foyer when she had to use the women's room. The washrooms were up a wide staircase. He nodded to several men he knew or had seen along the way, as he and Ruby walked to the stair. Everybody wanted to use the toilets before the band took their break. As they started up the stairs, Cleary spotted John and Lil, and Bill. Big Mike was with them, and two women Cleary had seen at least once at Thorbjorg's, all standing together at the top of the stairs.

Bill had a bottle in one hand, a joint in the other. He saw Cleary at the same time John did. Both yelled.

Cleary guided Ruby to them through the crowds on the steps.

Bill offered his bottle, and as Cleary took it, Ruby and John exchanged greetings. Lil put out the cigarette she was smoking with her shoe, asked Ruby if she didn't want to go with her to the washrooms.

"Wait!" Bill said. "I have to look the situation over." He gave no sign he remembered stopping for Ruby months before. He walked around her, looked her up and down.

Ruby blushed, assumed a model's pose, asked if he didn't want to look at her teeth.

"At your what?" Bill asked, with a leer.

Ruby blushed even more, and Bill roared.

Lil came to the rescue. "Come on," she said, leading Ruby away by the arm.

"I stopped for that chick in the spring, took her up to Thorbjorg's, remember?" Bill asked, of both Cleary and John, knowing that they were both there.

"That's when I met her," Cleary said.

The women standing with them didn't like the attention Ruby was getting even in her absence. One of them suggested to Bill that they get back to dancing. "Sure," Bill said, one step ahead of Big Mike and the two women as they all headed for the dancefloor.

"Be a good chance for Lil to tell you what she thinks of Ruby," John grinned.

Cleary mimicked Philip Whalen's, "Uhuh." "Looks pretty clear already," he said. "But I'll let you dance with her."

Ruby was surprised when John offered his arm to her as she and Lil returned. She gave Cleary a quick questioning look.

"John wanted a dance," Cleary said. "How could I refuse?"

Ruby slipped her arm into John's, then thought to look at Lil.

Lil put her arm around Cleary's by way of response.

Cleary liked the notion of "a Gathering of the Tribes," when he'd heard it, but thought any identification with the American Indian tribes was wrong, as he thought trends to Eastern thinking were wrong. We're our own tribe, Cleary thought, have to seek out our own beginnings, our own ancestors to venerate.

Cleary saw the long-haired and beaded on Haight Street as throwbacks to the Indo-European tribes that moved into India, the Middle East and Europe from central Asia around 3000 BC. Those from Europe who settled America came mostly from those peoples, after they had stopped moving, after the single language had broken down into many, after political borders and differentiated languages had encouraged hundreds of year's of inbreeding. What America made possible, he thought, was a re-creation of the original people, now that people bred beyond all the old lines. The same bloodlines, mixed again, made the people on the street more like those ancient peoples than any since.

Cleary thought a lot about the ancient peoples. He

didn't often have the chance to talk about them.

The road in had been muddy, even in the truck, after several days of steady rain. Cleary found several cars mired near the house. Going in, he found Thorbjorg and several others seated at the long table, kerosene lights lighting their faces.

He sat. The conversation had to do with setting up performances for one of the bands. When the conversation ended all sat several minutes in silence, before one of the band's road crew, an electrician, spoke. "What's that noise?"

Everyone at the table listened.

"I don't hear anything," someone said.

There was silence, as all tried to hear again whatever it was that the man had heard.

"What you hear is silence," Thorbjorg said. "You don't hear electricity."

It was briefly silent again while everyone verified what she had said.

"Living this way is great," one of the band said. "Wouldn't it be great if we could all live in the country, use kerosene light and woodstoves?"

Cleary tried to be gentler than he felt. This was one of those musicians who when they started to make money bought gold-plated rifles, brought them to Thorbjorg's, and had fired indiscriminately into the hills. They hadn't known that Willie One Bear was up there, trying to bring down a deer. Willie had been almost a year in an army hospital, recovering from wounds, when he got orders to return to Vietnam. He went AWOL. Found his way to Thorbjorg's. When the bullets hit near him, he hit the ground, firing back. The only thing that saved the band was that he was firing downhill, shot too high, and gave them a chance to hide.

"Who would cut the wood?" Cleary asked.

No answer. They knew they wouldn't, Cleary thought.

The man who wanted a woodstove yawned.

Somebody else said they wanted to raise horses.

"I'd love to ride into the city on a horse," Thorbjorg said. "Can you imagine crossing the bridge?"

Cleary had been reading of those Celts who had crossed Europe in both directions, mixed again with those cultures they found in southwest Asia. They had been horsemen. He had no trouble imagining Thorbjorg among them. He described the trappings they used on their horses, which included masks that made the horses appear antlered.

Thorbjorg liked the image. "We would fill the bridge," she said. "Thousands of us, on horses with antlers."

Uhuh, Cleary thought. He could only imagine it with Thorbjorg on one side of him, Bill on the other.

The door burst open. The woman who had been with Bill at the dance, soaked to the skin, her legs covered with mud, stood wild-eyed, the door open behind her, rain blowing in. She was out of breath, had been crying.

Cleary closed the door.

"Bill's going crazy," the woman said. She started to take off her wet clothes. "He got a letter from his mother. His father died."

Thorbjorg asked if the woman wanted something hot to drink.

"I ran all the way from the gate. I couldn't drive in. He's going crazy."

"Crazy how?" Cleary asked.

"We were having dinner. We were sitting at the

table, Bill and me, Big Mike and Mary Jane. All of a sudden he started to yell, picked up the dishes, threw them as hard as he could against the walls." As she talked she was back into it. She started to sob. "I was afraid he would come after me. I started to cry and he yelled at me, started to throw the dishes at me. I ran out of the house. I was sure he would follow me."

She had completely undressed, stood shivering and naked, crying before them.

Thorbjorg gave her someone's coat, her own chair. She had put on tea, she said.

"I didn't know where else to go," the woman said.

Relationships often go on a long time with few or no changes, with changes that are gradual, that happen almost without notice. One seldom wakes up to find that things are not what they seemed the night before.

Sometimes, however, one event does bring everything into a new focus, and even should that change be missed at the time, or unthinkingly made part of the whole, in retrospect, it is there to be seen for what it was, a turning point.

Cleary and Ruby both knew that their relationship, while held to a balance, had changed, the weight shifting from side to side. But it was slow in shifting. The facts that circumscribed the relationship were more or less constant. They lent to the relationship a sense of that constancy.

Had either of them thought about it, had Ruby or Cleary understood how near perfect their balance was, each might have recognized the potential in that balance for sudden imbalance.

The lock on the apartment's front door was one of those that could be made inoperable by key if it were properly set from inside. Ruby had not changed the original lock, but certain that someone besides herself and Cleary had a key that might someday be used, she took to setting the lock when alone. Cleary found it annoying that his key didn't always function, but understood Ruby's concern, and patiently waited for her to come down the stairs and let him in on those mornings he arrived before she'd reset the lock, which she usually did soon after waking.

Putting his key into the lock, Cleary wasn't certain it would open, wasn't certain that Ruby would be awake, even though it was late morning. She liked to sleep late.

The key turned, but not as it usually did. Cleary guessed, from the way the key did turn, that the lock had been set, but improperly, or partially, that something was slipping, and if he turned the key with sufficient pressure, it would open. It did. He reached over, rang the bell, announcing his arrival with the ring they had both agreed to use.

Thorbjorg's baby was soon to be born. The birth was to be an event, one Ruby had been anticipating, and Cleary was sure of her excitement. He took the steps two at a time, heard Ruby's voice calling his name as he climbed. He continued up the stairs. She called again, more intently. She thought he was still downstairs at the front door., he thought smiling.

At the top of the steps he could still hear her calling, apparently from the front window near her bed. As he moved forward, a man's face appeared, peeking through the open doorway. The man grinned. A shit-eating grin, Cleary thought.

Ruby stopped yelling and turned to see Cleary standing between her and the naked man whose clothes were beside hers on the floor beside her bed.

146

She was angry. "Why didn't you answer me?" She was embarrassed. "I thought the lock was set!" She was hurt. "This is terrible! You weren't coming this morning."

She started to cry. "You can't stay," she said. "You have to go."

Cleary couldn't tell who she was talking to. Neither could the naked man. His grin was starting to slide. He wasn't sure what was supposed to happen next.

"I'll come back later," Cleary said.

"Promise!" Ruby said, almost hysterical, sure he wouldn't.

"I'll come back," Cleary assured her. "I'll give you ten minutes."

The man was Cleary's height, younger, with long blond hair and a heavy mustache. Cleary turned back at the door to see him picking up his clothes. Ruby was sitting on the bed, crying, her head in her hands, talking to herself, still trying to understand how Cleary had opened the door.

Cleary looked at his watch as he reached the front door. The set was in place on the lock. He reset it. He would let himself in.

Cleary walked for five minutes up the street, turned, walked back.

He was angry. He was angry at himself for being angry. His inattentiveness, which he'd certainly been aware of, had brought on what it had to bring on. Ruby needed attentions he had chosen not to answer to. What could he expect? But he had expected more. That she had picked a stranger... Perhaps the man wasn't a stranger. Perhaps it all had been going on for some time, perhaps what he had taken for depression was already some inability to function as she had with him, because of a relationship with another.

Cleary was angry because he didn't want to be where he was. What did he care who Ruby fucked? If he had paid more attention to his own marriage, he wouldn't be there, would be at home, a clear and simple life. He would be thinking what he wanted to be thinking, not being dragged through someone else's emotions.

Cleary didn't ring the bell when he unlocked the door. He hoped the son-of-a-bitch was gone. He'd better be gone.

Ruby sat on the top step. He climbed the steps slowly.

"I'm glad you came back," she said.

"I said I would."

Ruby was wearing the dress she knew was his favorite, a full white skirt with a loose and open shirt top. Maybe she'd planned the whole thing, he thought. Maybe she wore it to show him how much she meant to him.

"I didn't want you to find out," she said.

"He's been here before?"

Ruby was quiet. Somehow she'd said too much. She started to cry. "I didn't want it to happen," she said.

"Didn't want what to happen?" he demanded.

"I didn't want another man. I wanted you. He's only been here twice before. I only met him a week ago."

"When does he come back?" Cleary asked.

"I told him I'd call him. But I won't. I want you."

"You just do what you think best," Cleary said.

"I love you, Cleary."

"I came to tell you that Thorbjorg started her labor. She sent Bill to tell me – he came by this morning before the sun came up. She thought the baby would be born before the sun set."

Ruby had become another person. "We should hurry! We can't miss it!"

As she looked into Cleary's face, she was suddenly back where she had been minutes before. "He doesn't mean anything to me, Cleary."

Cleary did his best to grin. "Does he want kids?"

Ruby blushed. "He has one. Back in Ohio. When his wife left him he came out here." She paused. "I want your baby, Cleary."

"Let's get out of here," Cleary said. He wanted to ask the man's name, but didn't.

Those around Thorbjorg had remarked on how as her pregnancy progressed she had become more beautiful. In the last weeks she had become more serene than most could tolerate.

"It's the acid," she finally said. "I take a little bit every day. Like vitamins."

Could she be believed? Even she knew that acid damaged chromosomes.

She winked at Cleary. "He'll be a superman."

Cleary wondered again who the father was. It had been spring. He remembered Bill carrying Thorbjorg to her cabin, but she had said there were others, that she didn't know who the father was. She had a good idea, he guessed.

Brautigan asked her where the baby had been conceived, clearly hoping for something to titillate his imagination.

"If I told you, you wouldn't believe it," she said, giving him exactly what he had hoped for.

Thorbjorg had chosen to have the baby in the space she knew best, rather than in the larger house. Cleary tried at one point to count how many were squeezed into the small cabin. There were too many, and they kept moving, coming and going between the two buildings.

When someone wondered aloud whether one usually had such a long labor, Ruby, who had been reading up on the subject, knowingly said that first labors were often long.

"How long has it been?" Cleary asked, trying to remember how long Marie had been in labor. It had been most of a day, he thought.

"The contractions began last night," Thorbjorg said. "After making love," she added.

Bill paged through a medical text. He flashed pictures of one birth deformity after another at Cleary. "The little bastard kicked my prick," he said, not taking his eyes from the book.

"It isn't my first," Thorbjorg said. "I started shooting speed when I had to give up the first."

Lil, who had brought the baby a silver cup without any engraving, suggested that she knew of a doctor who might be happy to come.

"Who'll pay him?" Cleary asked.

"He might come just to be here," John said.

"Promise him anything," Bill said. "If we don't pay him, he won't miss it."

There was a small table in one corner of the room where people had been putting gifts for the baby. To get to it you had to walk around Thorbjorg and those close to her. A new group came in, bearing gifts. Thorbjorg held up a small quilt.

Lil suggested to John that he go down to call the doctor.

"The baby will be fine," John said.

"The mother might need help," Lil said.

John looked over his shoulder at Lil, who sat

behind him. "If I go now, I might miss the whole thing."

Cleary offered to go. Thorbjorg heard him, broke off her talk with those around her long enough to say, "You stay, Cleary." She went on talking to the others.

Ruby and Cleary exchanged looks. He had no idea why Thorbjorg wanted him to stay.

John stood. "I have the number," he said, as he moved off.

In a whisper, Ruby asked Cleary why Thorbjorg wanted him to stay.

"I don't know," he said.

He tried to remember what Thorbjorg had said that night before the accident. She had said something about seeing more of him, but he couldn't come up with the exact words. Maybe there was something else she'd said.

The doctor arrived at sundown. John had stayed in Point Reyes, met him there, and guided him in. He timed Thorbjorg's contractions before his quick examination, assured her and all around her that everything was fine.

After the examination, the contractions were suddenly harder, closer together, and Thorbjorg was obviously feeling them as she hadn't before. Her water broke.

"His hands were cold," she said, between contractions.

No one needed the doctor to tell them that the baby was coming. The cabin was suddenly alive. Someone ran down to the large house, told everyone there.

Cleary woke Bill by shaking his foot.

All crowded around the bed to view the birth. Bill kept them from getting too close.

Thorbjorg lay with her legs apart, knees up, hips raised, and all watched as the baby's head became visible, watched as it emerged with a contraction that Thorbjorg later described as being like a huge orgasm.

It was a boy, as Thorbjorg had said it would be.

Cleary noted the exact time of the birth. Thorbjorg would want it.

The doctor waited for, then examined, the after-birth. He wanted to be sure it was all there. Thorbjorg, too, examined it – there were things that might be learned from it, she said.

As she lay with the baby on her chest, Cleary tried to compare the child's body to Bill's. The boy's face was much as Thorbjorg's own. There were similarities, he thought, but how could you know. He watched Bill's response to the baby. If it was his, Cleary determined, Bill didn't know it.

Most of the group left when the doctor did. Thorbjorg needed her rest, he said.

Thorbjorg was too high to sleep, speeding on her own adrenaline and hormones. She wanted to get up and move, clean her body. When she stood, she was light-headed, almost fell, but once on her feet, couldn't be stopped. Ruby and some of the other women stood round, helped her as she bathed.

Thorbjorg returned to a clean bed, lay with the baby in her arms.

"I want my own baby," Ruby whispered.

It wasn't clear when he left why Thorbjorg had wanted Cleary there. He was sure he would find out, sure it had to do with things to come.

———

Cleary wanted to live with the only child he had, he wanted to live with Laura. As near as he could tell, that meant that he and Marie should be together. He couldn't see why it shouldn't happen. He had good feelings for Marie. He probably even loved her. It didn't matter anymore, he thought. The life he had had with Marie and Laura was the life he still wanted.

Marie was not easily convinced that she wanted to live with Cleary. Too long had elapsed. She had had a taste of a life of her own, a life that had allowed her to heal some of her wounds. It didn't make sense to put herself back into it. Cleary hadn't moved in with Ruby, a situation he had even told her about, but there could easily be others she didn't know about. She didn't want to make the same mistake twice. Laura alone gave her reason to think seriously about a return to that earlier life. Cleary was Laura's father, and Laura deserved a life with her father, if that was in any way possible.

After several days of talk, Marie said she would return, would live with Cleary, a statement she questioned often in the days that followed as their future living arrangements were discussed. Ultimately Marie agreed to move to Sebastopol. She would live in the house that Cleary had rented. They would buy the car she had long wanted, to insure her mobility so far from her work and Laura's school, though Cleary promised he would deliver her and Laura each morning, arrange his schedule to pick them up each afternoon.

Marie and Cleary were together in his bed in the Sebastopol house. Marie was asleep, Cleary still awake, when the deputy came with the message for him.

"I have a message for Frank Cleary," the man said. "You should get a phone out here."

"I'm Cleary."

"Somebody named Ruby Rose was in an accident. Her car was totaled. She's in Marin General Hospital.

She wants you to be in touch."

"How bad is she hurt?"

The deputy saw a woman in a bathrobe move behind Cleary as he returned to his car. "I don't know how bad she's hurt. All I know is that Ruby Rose is in Marin General and wants you to be in touch."

The deputy got into his car. Cleary turned to Marie. "Ruby was in an accident. Her car was totaled. She's in the hospital," he said.

"What difference should it make to you?" Marie asked.

"I have to find out what happened," Cleary said.

"Read about it in the newspaper. If you go to see her," Marie said, "I'm leaving, for good."

"I'll just go into town, and call. I won't be more than an hour."

"If you go, I won't be here when you get back."

Cleary didn't believe her. She wasn't being rational. If she thought about it for a few minutes, he was sure she'd understand that.

Marie stood in the door, watched him get into the truck, start it and maneuver it around her new car in the narrow driveway. As the truck reached the road, she turned back into the house, walked from room to room turning on all the lights. She hesitated outside Laura's door, but went in, turned on the lights, woke Laura. She would be gone when Cleary returned.

Thorbjorg had come to Cleary's house in Sebastopol. The boy needed a name and it had not come to her. She asked Cleary if he would take acid with her, there, in his house, give her help in finding the boy's name.

"I want you to be his godfather," Thorbjorg said.

154

Cleary wasn't sure what that meant, but he had an idea, and that was enough. Like an uncle, he thought. "Sure." he said.

"Have you ever taken acid?" Thorbjorg asked.

He hadn't, he said. He could see the thought behind her question. She had taken acid all during her pregnancy. The likelihood was that it had in some way changed the boy's mind. If it had, to understand that mind, one had to have at least experienced the same perceptions.

Cleary had never wanted to change his perceptions. So what if nobody under thirty trusted him? He liked the world the way he saw it. Why not keep it that way?

The baby started to cry. Thorbjorg had taken him off one breast, changed to the other.

It made sense, Cleary thought, to Thorbjorg. If your mind put things together the way hers seemed to. Why not? he thought. Do I have anything else to lose?

The baby had to have a name, Cleary thought.

He had read how some native peoples sought out their own names, fasted in isolate places until they were visited, usually by an animal, who gave them their names. Thorbjorg wanted him to give the baby its name. Or they would find it together. She had come because she knew he would help her, Cleary thought.

Cleary said he would do it.

Thorbjorg reached for her black and white bag, took from it a tab of acid. "We'll split this one," she said. "You won't have a wild trip. You will go just far enough."

They each swallowed their halves. "It will come slowly," Thorbjorg said. "Just do what you must. And keep the baby in your mind."

While Thorbjorg sat with the baby, Cleary busied

himself with putting his things together.

He didn't want to be thinking about Ruby. He was supposed to be thinking about the baby.

He didn't know how much time had elapsed since he'd taken the acid. He felt he had to go outside. He had to see Loup.

When he looked into Loup's eyes he saw a dead man. It was like a photograph, a man in dark clothes, laying on the ground. Dead.

Tears came to his eyes. He wiped his eyes with the heels of his hands. "We'll go on a trip, Loup. We'll go somewhere."

He needed to see Thorbjorg, wanted to run his fingers through the child's hair. It wasn't a child yet, he thought, it didn't have hair.

He was standing in front of the chair, his hand on the baby's head, Thorbjorg's hand on his, when they heard a car in the driveway.

Cleary went to the door. It was Ruby. "Go out to meet her," Thorbjorg said.

"Who's here?" Ruby asked.

"Thorbjorg. We took acid. We're naming the baby."

The look on Ruby's face was one he hadn't seen there before. Maybe it was the acid. Maybe it was Ruby. She had the kind of look she might if she were on a mountain, gazing into the distance.

"I want to see the baby, and then I'll take the lamb. I don't want to spoil your trip."

Cleary walked behind Ruby into the house. Thorbjorg and the baby were in the chair that Ruby used those days when just back from Europe. He couldn't see Ruby's face. Thorbjorg smiled up at her for several seconds, before Ruby turned. She was smiling when she turned, but Cleary thought it was a strange smile. It was as though she were in a familiar room, but surrounded by strangers.

As Cleary handed the lamb to Ruby, he felt that it would die. She was taking it to its death. He didn't tell her.

Ruby waved as she backed what she said was a borrowed car down the driveway.

Thorbjorg was in the doorway when Cleary turned. "His name is coming," she said.

Cleary turned. He looked out to the grass on the hill before him, saw it moving as he hadn't before. His eyes moved beyond the hill and the road, to the sky, a shimmering blue sky.

Egil, he thought. "E, g, i, l," he spelled.

"He was a wild man," Thorbjorg said. "A poet."

The man who owned Thorbjorg's place wanted to sell it. If he did sell, she was sure she'd have to find another place, that she couldn't go on living where she was. "It isn't time for me to move," she said.

She took up her shotgun, walked to the gate, to the sign the man had put up making public his intent to sell.

She fired until there was little left of the sign. She left what there was for the man to see. It wasn't time to sell. He would understand.

Cleary felt it was time for him to move. He would come back, because Laura was there, but he felt he had to return to Missouri, to touch it, gain what he could from those beginnings.

He told John his plans.

"Sounds like a good idea to me," John said. Moving was in the air. Change. It seemed many were moving. John himself would move soon. "If you're gone long enough," he said, "I'll have my new place when you get back."

Marie didn't like the idea, but was willing to let Cleary store his things on her porch, once he'd explained that John too would be moving.

Laura helped Cleary carry the things from the truck, and together they stacked them against the wall, as Marie suggested. Laura wanted to go to Missouri with her father. Except for the fact that he had no idea how long he might be gone, Cleary liked the idea. Marie said no immediately. She was afraid that Cleary would never return, that he'd gladly trade his things for his daughter. Her father could see her when he came back.

When they kissed goodbye, both father and daughter knew, however long, it would be the longest they'd ever been apart.

"Give Grandma and Grandpa big kisses." Laura gave Loup a big hug. "Don't forget to feed Loup."

"We'll take care of each other," Cleary said.

Cleary hadn't planned to call Ruby. He had already reached Sacramento when he did. He wanted space between them, didn't want to be so near that she might talk him into coming by to see her before he left.

"I threw the I Ching," Ruby said. "I got the Wanderer. I'm going to New Mexico." The man Cleary had found in her apartment was driving, he had friends out of Santa Fe. "Write me care of Mother," she said.

It would be hard to explain to his folks, Cleary thought, what wasn't clear even to himself.

Loup rode on the front seat beside Cleary. Shotgun, Cleary thought. He was somebody to talk to. He hadn't talked to Loup for a long time.

Nobody in the family really wanted to hear what had happened. It was over, what was done was done. The lesson was that if you were blood you might do what others shouldn't. They didn't like it, and hopefully you wouldn't make the same mistakes again, but blood is blood.

Cleary was sure he'd made mistakes. They hadn't been recognizable when he'd made them, only afterwards. Hind sight, he thought.

When he learned that his sister, Beverly, had separated from her husband, a man Cleary had never cared to understand, Cleary better understood his parent's view. They couldn't be involved, couldn't go in all the directions that their children might take them.

Beverly lived in Detroit. She wanted to come home. Cleary suggested that first night that he might go and get her. His mother thought it a good idea. His father wasn't at all sure he wanted both of his children so close. He would think on it.

Cleary tried to imagine where Laura might someday lead him. He laughed. If she was anything like he was, and she was, it wouldn't be easy. He didn't want to think about the influence Marie and her mother would have on Laura, didn't want to think where that would lead him. This was the negative side, Cleary thought, family not spoken of. You didn't want to speak, even when you knew, because no matter how much you knew it all to be true and the way it was, you wished it weren't, wanted to think rather of the way it ought to be.

Beverly had her things packed and ready, but they couldn't leave. The night Cleary arrived Detroit came under siege and martial law was declared.

They watched it all on TV, from the floor of her apartment. Cleary wouldn't sit in the chairs, heard around him the gunfire, single shots and machine gun fire, heard the screeching tires, sirens, knew the floor to be the safest place.

Coverage of the event showed it to be complex. Although Blacks were said to have instigated and initiated the affair, there were whites with crew cuts and a military manner arrested.

Cleary became convinced as he watched that the U.S. government was behind the trouble, that it was an event planned to draw out and eliminate militant Blacks and their leaders. It had worked before. It would work again.

It was part of a larger plan, Cleary felt. It was reported that the Quebec Free French wanted to separate Quebec from the rest of Canada, that they were somehow in league with those in the States, and it was all made to appear that the whole of the northeastern U.S. would be cut off from the rest of the country. The situation allowed for, demanded, they said, military law. They were tightening it all up. Those in power wanted to stay in power.

There would be no alternatives.

The first thing Cleary's mother said to him when he returned from Detroit was that a woman named Ruby had called. She left a phone number, asked that he call as soon as possible.

Ruby didn't wait for the call she guessed Cleary wouldn't find time to make. "New Mexico was terrible. The lamb was killed in one of those cyanide traps they set for coyotes. And my friend had another woman in New Mexico that he forget to tell me about. What were you doing in Detroit? Were you involved in any of the trouble there?"

"No," Cleary said. "We watched it on TV."

"I wanted you to know where I was, Cleary." Ruby

said she would call again when she found a place and would give him the address.

The Kansas City TV coverage of the violence in Detroit did not include much of the coverage they had watched in Detroit. While the Blacks were shown as they were arrested, there were no longer whites among them. It was too obvious, Cleary thought. In their initial eagerness to show it all, the cameramen had gone too far for someone. Those in power knew the viewers would believe what they saw. You simply couldn't show them too much, too much confused them. You had to keep the party line simple, Cleary thought.

Raymond, Cleary's cousin, asked Cleary if he could help with moving to his new place. It was in one of those valleys that came up off the river. Fields had been cleared, openings made in the trees.

"Looks like a good place," Cleary said.

"If a fellow wanted to build a little cabin back in here, he could probably find a place," Raymond said, pointedly.

"Nobody would know you were there," Cleary said, letting it go. But it might come to that, he thought. "I'll be heading west again," Cleary said. "I don't want to get too much space between Laura and me."

Raymond had married a girl from Kentucky when he was twenty-one, and she fifteen. Cordelia – he called her Dee – was thirty-two now. She had four kids, the fifth on its way. Raymond worked where he could. Dee kept a big garden, helped feed the animals, besides keeping up the house, chasing after the kids while she tried to cook and wash and mend clothes.

Cleary had a hard time imagining another girl in Dee's place. He wondered, if Raymond hadn't married Dee, might he have found some other who would have put up with what she did, no matter where she was from?

Time was against them, Cleary decided. Nobody seemed able to see the joy of spending their days working at their own life. Men or women. They all seemed set on having it all done for them, having it all ready made, and delivered, ready to go.

He had hoped it wasn't true, but he saw the same sickness creeping into Missouri that he had seen in California. People didn't do things for themselves. Most didn't raise their own food. Few built their own houses or sewed their own clothes. When they raised animals, the animals were pets, not to eat.

People couldn't even amuse themselves anymore. When those very people he had learned music from got together to play, it was no longer part of their daily life, but rather some kind of staged event.

Returning from times away, you found that things weren't as they had been, as you had carried them in your absence. Maybe things had never been quite as you saw them, but you never realized how much it was so until you went away and then returned.

Returned, because you were family, however changed the family found you, there would be a place, but it was a place in the family, not in the community itself. You had no life in the place beyond the family because you didn't, couldn't really, interact on a greater level. You brought back to the community ways of doing things that were no longer, if they had ever been, the way things were done. You began to understand, as Jesse James and others returning from that or any war had, that it might all be easier if you weren't there, no embarrassment, to the few who felt obliged to try and deal with you.

Your first choice gone, you had to make another. If you could still go back to wherever it was that you had just come from, however much this second choice too seemed inconsistent with who you thought you were, you might. Or you might continue to move as you found yourself moving. There wasn't really a choice. You had to be as you were, move as you could.

For Cleary, Raymond's and Bill's understanding was the closest to his own that he was likely to find. Little John, though from another place, was from the same time, understood enough to make it work. They had moved through the same thinking – despite the fact, as Cleary knew, that thinking has little to do with anything beyond thought.

There were no really close women with Marie gone. That she had had such close contact, that they had known one another so well for so long, that they had experienced all they had together, had brought her as close as anyone might ever be. He could see no one who might be as close, though he hoped there might be. He couldn't see living his life without a woman.

Ruby fit into it somewhere, he thought. She filled some need. But there was so much she wasn't connected to, so much he was that she wasn't.

Ruby had called while Cleary was out. She left her address, a phone number. He would call her, he thought. When he was ready. And when he returned to California he'd go to see her. Maybe I'll understand what I didn't. Maybe, he thought.

Cleary called Ruby from Reno. He had driven all night and though she sounded glad to hear he was on his way back, glad that she would see him again, Cleary thought she sounded a bit preoccupied. He told himself he just needed sleep. He asked for directions to her place, said he didn't know his way around the roads and streets between Mill Valley and San Rafael as he might. As he later thought about it, he had been awake. Once she had told him where she was, Ruby had pinned him down as to just when he might arrive.

Ruby had grown large in his mind as he drove west. Was it simply that she was there, a woman he might relate to, because he had already, or was there more to it? Was she meaningful in some way that he hadn't explored, meaningful in a way that only now, with the perspective Missouri had given him, allowed him to appreciate her for what she had been all along?

Maybe, he thought, it's been so long I've forgotten what she's really like, have created a woman that doesn't really exist. But he did remember. I'm some kind of optimist, he thought, don't remember the bad as bad as it was, remember the good better than it was. He laughed to himself.

"Maybe I need some advice, Loup," he said.

Loup gave him one of those "get serious" looks. Cleary's grin faded as he thought more about Loup. The dog tuned him into basics like nothing else could. There was one reality, the one right there in front of you. It was the only reality that finally mattered. If you got into thinking, it took you where you wanted to go, maybe where your mind needed to go, for whatever reason, but it finally had nothing to do with what was really there in front of you.

Cleary remembered how often he had told Laura to "pay attention." It was time for him to pay attention.

He would have to have a place to live, he thought. Do I want to live with Ruby? He laughed to himself. Loup looked at him again. You'll know when you get there, he told himself. Missouri seemed to have done strange things to him. Or maybe he just needed sleep.

It was still light enough to see the street signs when he arrived in Mill Valley. He drove into the center of town, as Ruby had directed, then followed her directions into the hills north of Mill Valley itself. As she had said he would, he found a mailbox on the road, numbered and with a blue flower, beside a stairway that led up to the house.

He wasn't sure what she was driving, and looked carefully at the cars parked along the street, thinking that he might spot which was in fact hers. He noted a truck much like John's parked half a block above the steps, but found a parking spot before he reached it, passed it off as belonging to someone else as he hurried up the steps.

There was a quietness to Ruby as she answered the door that struck Cleary as unusual, even before he saw John, with earphones in his ears, his back turned to the door, listening and dancing to something on Ruby's new stereo.

Ruby smiled a smile that reminded him of smiles his mother had given him when he'd returned from school to find her busy with her own things. She took his shoulders in her hands as she kissed him. A gentle kiss.

Cleary didn't want to consider why John was there. John was his friend, and he was happy to see him. He crossed the room, came up behind him and tapped him on the shoulder, even as his stomach felt those strange feelings one's stomach sometimes feels in circumstances beyond one's control.

John turned, expecting Ruby, and reddened some, Cleary thought, seeing him, but he put his arms around Cleary, and the two hugged as two bears might, as they always had.

John's voice was loud, he spoke over music he alone could hear. "I'll be right with you – after this song," he said. He turned back to the machine, danced on. Cleary glanced at the record cover John had propped up. The Grateful Dead's "American Beauty."

Ruby was right behind Cleary, and when he turned, he took her quickly in his arms. She tried to speak as he moved to kiss her, but she wasn't fast enough. As he pressed his mouth to hers, he felt her fingers tighten on his shoulders.

Ruby wanted to speak. She had to speak. "John and I are going to have a baby," she said.

All Cleary could think was that he hadn't been paying attention. He should have seen it coming from even the few clues he had. He hadn't known himself, hadn't anticipated the willingness he now seemed to have to finally accept Ruby. Now that she had gone on without him.

Cleary turned to John. Where was John?

John had turned, saw Cleary turn to him, guessed from the expression on his face and the way he stood that Ruby had told him she was pregnant. John reached for the stereo, switched the music from earphones to loudspeakers. The music was too loud. He turned it down.

John grinned. Caught in the act, he thought. "Ruby tell you about the baby?"

It was Cleary's turn to grin. "She did," he said. He turned back to Ruby, asked, "When is it due?"

"We just found out," Ruby said. There was a peacefulness to her that Cleary didn't remember. She was happy, and had it not been the strained situation it was, she would have bubbled over with her good feelings. She was holding back. There was no doubt in anyone's mind that she would have the child.

Everything happens the way it is supposed to happen, Cleary reminded himself. His own way was suddenly clear. Clear and empty, he thought. "Great news," he said, trying hard.

Both John and Ruby felt great relief when he said it. Both moved to him, and the three of them hugged as they had once before.

Ruby's enthusiasm broke free. "I'm so happy," she said, almost apologetically.

Cleary didn't want apologies. "When, exactly, is it due?"

Ruby explained that the doctor felt she was seven weeks pregnant, and then, standing at her wall calendar, as though she herself didn't believe what the doctor had told her, counted off the remaining weeks. She had already marked the day.

Cleary couldn't help but realize that Ruby and John had found one another almost immediately after she'd returned to California. Why hadn't he thought of the possibility in Missouri, or on the way back? He hadn't been paying attention, but rather letting his mind go where it might.

Cleary wanted to ask what had happened to Lil, but he wanted to be discreet, wanted no bad feelings. "So where will you be living? he asked, addressing the two of them as though they were together, a single identity.

They weren't, and the question was one that neither wanted to think about. It was the dark cloud on

167

the horizon, Cleary realized.

"I'm still living with Lil," John said. "I've framed up the house, put a roof on it, and we're more or less camping in it. Lil put all her things in storage."

"I'll live here," Ruby said, adding, "until I can convince John to come live with his baby."

She had all the aces, Cleary thought. Both she and John knew that the child was what John had always wanted, and Ruby was sure that he would do what he had to do, however long it took.

That John hadn't already separated from Lil, hadn't moved in with Ruby, led Cleary to wonder if he would. Cleary had seen for himself how hard it was to leave a woman you really cared for, remembered Raymond's thought that a man seldom leaves his woman. If Lil wasn't herself ready to let it go, Cleary wondered, would it happen?

John asked, "And what are you doing, Cleary? Where are you putting down?"

Cleary grinned. "Well, I was thinking to move in here," he said. He saw from the immediate response that his attempt at humor had gone too far. John feared as much, knew the statement to be true, and didn't want Cleary to enter into it, didn't want to feel that Cleary had any influence in his choices. Ruby's cards were already too good, exerting more pressure than he wanted.

"But I can see," Cleary went on, "that I'll have to rethink my position." Loup's expression came back to him.

Ruby was quick to pick up on her advantages. "You can stay here, if you like." She turned to John, and embarrassed at her own thoughts, blushed, but said, "At least you wouldn't have to worry about my getting pregnant."

168

John didn't like any of it. He put his earphones back on, before Cleary said he would stay at Thorbjorg's until he found another place. Cleary shouted it again, then asked John when they could get back to work.

They would find a new balance, Cleary thought, a balance that kept together what should stay together. It would be Ruby, who knew so well what she wanted, and was so determined to have it, who would set the balance. She would accept nothing short of her desires, unless her own thinking changed.

———————

Maybe it was because he was at Thorbjorg's that Cleary felt things speeding up. It felt as though too many were out on the edge, out there taking chances where in normal times people don't, and it made a difference. Most found themselves in situations they hadn't prepared themselves for, and being there, on the edge, was at best strange to them. To others it was deadly.

People were dying, and for no good reason, that Cleary could think of, except the fact that they were middle-class kids with middle-class values and virtually no knowledge or experience of anything resembling where they found themselves. They took chances they didn't know they were taking, didn't know the odds, or enough to worry about beating the odds.

They weren't paying attention.

One man Cleary knew was killed when he jumped from the second story of a house being raided. The jump didn't kill him, but the man who jumped on top of him did. Another man, who carried a gun he didn't know well, threw the gun onto his bed as he left his room, thinking he wouldn't need it, and the gun went off when it hit. The bullet blew a hole in his chest. A woman carrying drugs was driving on the freeway when a State Patrol car pulled in behind her, signaled her to stop. She had to get rid of the drugs she felt in the panic that must have seized her, and she swallowed them, died of an overdose.

There were stabbings, shootings, but they were intentional.

A man who often visited Thorbjorg's, a man who lived in the hills of Marin, fed himself with what he could find or hunt, told of discovering the body of a woman strangled and thrown over the road's shoulder into the brush below.

The people coming through Thorbjorg's began to change. They weren't all flower children anymore, but included people who needed to get out of the city to breathe easy, many either cleaning up habits, or on the run. There were tensions that hadn't been there before. It reached a point finally that Thorbjorg let it be known that the place was filled, that there was no room for anyone else.

One day in Thorbjorg's absence, a couple who had stayed briefly months before returned. They were told that Thorbjorg wanted no one to move in. Instead of waiting for her return to plead their case, the man moved his and his wife's things into a room used for storage, piled the stored things beside the building —except for those stored things he incorporated into his own things.

When the others saw their things in the man's use they had to decide what use of their things they would allow. The man unhappily put into the storage pile, or gave to their owners, those things he was denied use of.

Thorbjorg returned and after speaking with the man's wife, decided that theirs was reason enough for them to stay. Days later, the man left without his wife, but took with him numerous things that weren't his to take. Word traveled quickly of the incident, and the man's whereabouts were discovered.

Thorbjorg prodded the man awake the next morning with her shotgun, stood by with the gun as he loaded all that was not his into the back of a truck she had borrowed.

The incident didn't end there. The man came up one night to Thorbjorg's cabin, to find her apparently asleep in her chair at her table, her kerosene light turned way down. The man pulled a knife.

From the shadows, where the man had missed them, Big Mike cocked his revolver, asked if he should kill the man, and Bloody Bill replied, "It might wake the baby."

"Surely you understand," the man said, "I only intended to frighten Thorbjorg."

"Surely you understand," Bill said, "that the next time we see you, wherever, you're a dead man."

The police in the area also seemed to change. They no longer saw themselves as locals, but took on the militant posture of the federal government. They took more note of what was going on, began to follow the bikers and others as they passed through Point Reyes, or Stinson, to see where they were going, harassing them, checking paperwork. By California law, a vehicle could be stopped for on-road inspection, and Cleary and others were stopped again and again for such infractions as faulty windshield wipers.

One morning those two people still at Thorbjorg's, one of them a man high on acid, the other a young girl, found that the place was being raided by horsemen who slipped down over the hills, surrounded the buildings. They searched the place, found nothing. Those who searched Thorbjorg's cabin left her shotgun, opened and empty, its shells stood on end beside it, on her bed. They took with them, she swore, her only pair of black silk underpanties.

One Sunday afternoon a man was found beaten along the road near Point Reyes, and a police car drove up the dirt road into Thorbjorg's yard to investigate. There were four officers in the car. When they pulled into the yard they discovered the thirty-odd choppers lined up there. They didn't get out of the car, even when beer cans were hurled at it.

Marie was dating a fellow teacher. Laura had filled Cleary in on who the man was, had said that she liked him. "He's fun," she had said. Cleary asked if Laura thought she could live with the man if her mother wanted to marry him.

"I don't think it's that far along," Laura said.

"Would you mind if it were?"

"No," Laura said. "I might even like it."

When it came time for Laura to buy her mother a Christmas present, she asked Cleary to help her find it. "You'll have to help pay for it, too."

"What do you want to buy?" Cleary asked.

"A dress."

"Any special kind?"

"A nice dress. One that makes her prettier," Laura explained.

They went to several stores before they found something they both liked. It was a little wilder than what Marie usually wore, a little brighter. When Cleary asked how they should wrap it, Laura said she didn't want to wrap it.

"She needs it before Christmas," Laura said. "I

want her to have it on her next date."

"Does she know you're buying a dress?" Cleary asked, trying to understand.

"She doesn't know what I'm buying," Laura said. "I want her to have a new dress, one that makes her prettier. If she has a prettier dress, maybe she'll get married again sooner."

"I think you've got it all figured out," Cleary said.

Marie told Cleary just after Christmas that she would marry again when the divorce waiting period was over. Cleary laughed. Marie was hurt, until he explained that Laura had engineered the whole thing. Marie blushed, said she didn't know what to think.

Big Mike was one of those people who grew on you. Once you got beyond the racism and the confrontational approach he used to greet most he didn't know, he was a simple man who took life mostly as it came. He had what he referred to at different times as "common sense" or "Yankee ingenuity." He was from northern Maine, French-Canadian, had worked at lumbering, in the potato fields, and later as a fisherman, operating his own boat alone for days at a time in the North Atlantic, a job he gave up because the girl he was briefly married to couldn't handle her worries while he was out in bad weather. Instead of waiting for the divorce that would give his wife everything, including his unpaid-for boat and house and chopper, he had taken his gun and the chopper and had headed west, leaving his wife and her family behind to figure out the finances.

Sitting beside Cleary on the curb in front of a Bolinas bar, Mike extolled the virtues of Maine. He said he missed the winters, the deep snow and cold.

"I've seen drifts almost as high in May back there as they are in the Sierras," he said.

It was May, and Cleary attributed the gathering he'd found in the bar to the weather, could think of no other reason all these folks might have come together. The pool tables were crowded, the bar lined and backed up. There were even people trying to dance to the jukebox. The only sensible thing, he and Mike had decided, was to bring your beer out into the street, drink it there.

Cleary had noticed Lil among the dancers. He'd looked for Little John, but hadn't seen him. Sooner or later he'd talk to Lil, find out what was happening at home. He had seen John the day before, and John had had nothing to say on the subject in the several hours they'd worked. John had talked mostly about the new large paintings he was doing on paper, which he wanted to mount as Japanese scrolls. He was using simple lines, he said, both delicate and bold, and color, to render, hundreds of times larger than they were, small growing things. He had said nothing about Ruby, and Cleary, though he wanted to, didn't ask.

"What we need," Mike grinned, "is a pitcher."

Cleary's beer was empty. He stood. "I'll bring one back," he said.

"Just whistle," Mike said. "I need to take a little walk." He too stood as Cleary went back into the bar.

The only place Cleary saw where he might actually get to the bar was in the back. As he moved through the dancers, Lil saw him, swung by him, and still in time with the pounding music, said, "Ruby's up at the house, with John. She's giving him the ultimatum."

Cleary said nothing, hardly hesitated. Maybe, he thought, as he moved on toward the bar, I'll swing up there later. He was sure Lil would need a ride.

———————

John's interest in Ruby was the child, his child. He told Ruby this, arranged with her to partake as much as possible in those last weeks of her pregnancy. He would help her through the birth, which she had decided would be a doctor-assisted home birth. He would do whatever he could after the birth. He wanted to share with her the experience of the child, despite the fact that they weren't going to be living together.

Ruby's focus narrowed to the baby, and however much she might later consider her and John's arrangement, it was what she could salvage at the moment, and took it for a foothold, hoping it might all blossom after the birth. Once the baby was born, Ruby knew there was always the chance that with a growing attachment to the child, John might reconsider, might want the closeness of a real parenting couple.

Cleary had come to feel that the past was past, that whatever he did next, whoever he might find himself with, would come from in front of him, and not from behind. Ruby had become a friend, the friend he had told Marie she was, and he wanted for her, and for John, whatever they felt was best for themselves.

———————

Cleary saw John first, sitting in the kitchen, looking at his glass, and as he moved toward him Lil's movement in the doorway above caught his eye. She was wearing one of her most seductive nighties, but her expression wasn't in keeping with it. She was working at changing her mood, maybe John's as well. Lil waved, and Cleary passed beneath her.

"What's up?" John asked, looking up.

"That's what I came to find out," Cleary said. "What happened?"

John picked up the bottle. Pouring Cleary a glass of the whiskey, he said, "The baby died."

Cleary didn't move.

"The baby was alive, and then as it was born, it strangled. Got caught up in the cord."

Cleary moved slowly for his glass, picked it up. He wanted to know why, how it could have happened. "There was nothing the doctor could do?"

"It was a boy," John said.

Cleary drank down his glass. "The doctor?" he asked again.

"It was the wrong doctor," John said. "Somebody else might have saved him, or realized what was happening before it happened. This guy didn't."

"Who was he?"

"A home birth specialist," John said bitterly.

"How's Ruby?" Cleary asked.

"Unhappy," John said.

Cleary couldn't help but think of how understated that had to be, how absolutely wild in her fury and agony Ruby had to be. He himself wanted the doctor before him, wanted to tear the man limb from limb.

And where was John?

Some part of John was dead.

"We went on the mountain this morning," John said. "We found a place to bury him."

Cleary walked to the window, stood looking out at the eucalyptus leaves turning in the evening breeze. For some reason he thought of Laura.

Lil came down the ladder, into the kitchen. "You'd better get your muffler fixed," she said.

Cleary turned. Lil had changed into her jeans. She stood behind John, her hands on his shoulders, rubbing them.

Cleary reached for the bottle. He remembered Thorbjorg's prophecy. "Did you ever tell Ruby..." he began.

John looked up into Cleary's eyes. He knew what Cleary was about to ask. "I never told anybody but you," he said.

"Told what?" Lil asked.

Neither Cleary nor John responded. Lil understood that she would never know. How important could it be?

Ruby said later that the last time she had gone to John's house she remembered a dream as she walked in. In the dream she found the path down to the house lined with tombstones. She hadn't stopped to look at them, to read what they said, had felt the chill of fear and wanted to get into the house. When she got into the house, it was changed. The rooms were different, and there was someone else's furniture there.

Lil alone had been there when John died.

Cleary heard the story several times. Lil and John had been to a party in the city. John had been drinking hard, had taken some kind of drugs, Lil didn't know what, and he needed to come home, but didn't want to. She had insisted, but worried about his ability to drive, had suggested she would drive. He wouldn't get into the truck until she agreed he would drive. They made it home. They argued all the way, she said, about whether she was trying to control his life. In the house he hadn't wanted to go immediately to bed. She insisted. He needed to go to bed. He'd been working inside on the west end of the house with the ladder, had left it there, and instead of moving it back to the finished upper bedroom, had climbed it where it stood. The argument continued as he walked the center beam from the west end toward the bedroom. Lil didn't remember what she said, but in the center of the big room, John had stopped, turned to her, said "Fuck you," and lost his balance as he turned to go on. His head hit the stove when he fell. Lil stood several seconds staring at him as he lay there before she started to scream. She didn't know how long she screamed. The closest neighbor heard her, came up to find her standing there. He checked John's pulse. John was dead.

It was all coming to an end. It was happening as Thorbjorg had said it would. Cleary knew that it wasn't over, that he hadn't passed through it all. It didn't feel over. He couldn't help but think of Ragnarok, the last great battle between the gods and the giants. Only the children of the gods would survive. And someone to tell the tale, Cleary thought.

Cleary didn't know what would happen next.

Some of the children would survive.

Laura was already headed for a new life. Marie's plans were to move south when she remarried. Her new husband-to-be wanted to return to the area he'd grown up in, and both he and Marie had lined up work for the fall.

Cleary didn't like the plan. It would put Laura beyond his reach, unless he too moved south. He couldn't imagine it. He understood that Marie's life had to go where it would, however his own and Laura's might be affected. He knew he couldn't expect Marie to concern herself with his problems. But he didn't like it.

He could see Laura a month in summer, the

divorce had said, visitation beyond that as could be arranged. However it was arranged, there was no reason to stay where he was, Cleary thought.

With John's death, Cleary had gone fully into landscaping. He didn't like it. It would be easy to leave. Leaving was in the air. He had camped at Thorbjorg's long enough, stayed because it was a place to stay, and he had no other. There had been reasons to stay, but they were no longer there.

Most at Thorbjorg's felt it was time to move. Some were planning caravans. Others were headed for communes in Oregon, New Mexico, Colorado. They were getting ready to spread the word. Cleary didn't want to move with them. He had to connect in his own way. He didn't think there was a promised land, had never knowingly followed anyone anywhere. Cleary just wanted to survive.

John had had a funeral. Lil organized a small group of people who had gone onto the mountain, chanted Buddhist chants, had given John's ashes to the wind. It had all been done as John wanted, Lil assured Cleary. If it had been, Cleary thought, there was in John's connection to Buddhism a part of John that he hadn't seen. In life, if John was a Buddhist, it had been there in the way he saw and did things, wasn't formal or rigid. Cleary had found the funeral formal, saw in it an institutionalized ritual too like the Christian churches he had known. It felt too much like hierarchy. Ritual only worked, Cleary thought, when it grew out of the moment, wasn't left over from the last time it was used.

It wasn't the kind of funeral Cleary would have given John. It was too quiet, too easy. The bluejays that flew through in the middle of it all had given it the only note it had, Cleary felt.

Like his father had always said, the funeral was

really for those left behind. It had to work for them. They had to know that whoever it had been was gone.

––––––––––––––

Thorbjorg never said who the man was. It was old business. He had showed up in the afternoon while she was gone. The man waited. No one knew him, and several asked why he was there, a question few ever asked. There was something about the man that made all who saw him uneasy.

Thorbjorg returned in an old flatbed truck, a 30's Ford, just at sunset. The man was nowhere around when all gathered around the truck, and no one thought of him as they examined the truck, which was to be used by some of those leaving, and talk went to how best use it.

Only later did all remember that the man had been there somewhere, that he had chosen to stay out of sight.

Cleary wondered, when it was over, whether Thorbjorg had known what was to happen, and if she had, why she said nothing, why she went as always to her cabin, without help, let it happen as it did. If she had known, he concluded, she wanted it to happen.

She left the boy in the kitchen, where he played beneath the big table. She would be back, she said, and one of the other women kept her eye on him, was checking his diaper when she heard the shots.

The man had been waiting for Thorbjorg. Cleary guessed that when she came through the door she had seen him, seen the white dog, Huginn, dead on her floor. The man went for her, tried to hold her, but she was too strong, too intent on getting through the room, to its far side, where she knew the loaded shotgun stood.

180

The first shot hit the man low. It was either a quick shot, Cleary guessed, or aimed at the man's genitals. It was the only shot at that range, the others obviously fired as she backed away.

The man's body lay on the floor amidst the scattered furniture, near Huginn, when Cleary and the others reached the cabin. Thorbjorg was reloading her shotgun. There was no emotion on her face.

"It's time to leave," she said. "It's time for me to leave," she corrected.

Thorbjorg ordered the cabin stripped of its hangings by two of the women, asked a third to gather the baby's things, as she put together the few things she would take. She said as she worked that she was leaving Egil, that she would return for him. She said it to no one in particular, said it for all to hear.

It all happened quickly, Thorbjorg alone beyond the shock the others felt. She poured kerosene from her lamps onto the man's body before anyone could think to object. She lighted a full book of matches, threw it onto the man, and all left as the black smoke filled the room.

She didn't wait with the others to watch the cabin burn. She walked down toward the house. Cleary was behind her. She stopped at her car, put her things into it. She wasn't going into the house. She wouldn't say goodbye.

"I'll find him," she said.

She got into the car, started it, then opened the door. "Take this for Egil," she said, handed Cleary the shotgun.

———————

By noon, most of the trucks were gone. Those who were still there wanted to return the place to the shape it had been in when Thorbjorg had first found it.

Cleary could only guess at how it had been. It would have to look like they'd never been there.

The 30's Ford made several trips to the dump.

There was, Cleary thought, reason enough to cover some of their tracks. Thorbjorg's cabin had burned to the ground. Poking through the ashes, Cleary saw to it that nothing remained to tell any of its stories.

Bill and Big Mike rode in at the very end of it. They had a bottle. They had run into trucks everywhere that day, they said, had talked to several. Some had whispered of the night before.

"The guy was probably a cop," Bill said. He liked the idea. "Maybe he was even a Fed." He liked that idea even better.

"Could be," Cleary said. "She left Egil, said she'd be back, would find him. Man had to have friends she was worried about."

Bill laughed. "Bring the fuckers on," he said.

He handed Cleary the bottle. Bill was sorry he hadn't been there, Cleary thought.

"It's time for a party," Bill said. "Time to blow the place wide open."

"We've been telling everybody to meet up in Bolinas, at the bar," Big Mike said.

Cleary said he would be there.

As the two choppers moved out, up the road, those few still with Cleary decided that enough was enough, said their goodbyes, and made for their trucks.

Cleary and Loup made one last round, walked through the house, the outbuildings, walked again up to what was left of the burned cabin.

Egil was on Cleary's mind. What would happen to Egil? Thorbjorg hadn't said who should take him, and one of the women had, along with two other kids whose father had disappeared and whose mother was in jail.

Was that how it was supposed to go? Cleary thought about being the boy's godfather. Thorbjorg had intended something else. She had said she wanted Cleary at the birth so he would be there from the beginning. She had never said how it was all supposed to happen, but she knew.

By not telling what she knew, Cleary thought, she let you think it was your own idea.

Pulling up the first hill, Cleary almost looked back, but he glanced at Loup, who was looking straight ahead.

Pay attention, Cleary thought.

———————

Gathered there on the single street of a small town, they were like bees that Cleary had seen in the woods swarm before they broke apart. They were a tribe, but he knew them too well to think of them as the tribal folk he wished they were.

Most seemed dressed for the occasion, wore their wildest clothes, all of their feathers and beads. And the trucks, like horses in another time, were decked out to carry the spirit of it all, as well as their riders.

It was the beginning of a new time, and everyone knew it. They would take what they had learned with them, whether they went as a group or alone. They were what they had become, and they were different. That difference would be felt wherever they went. Because the spirit of that difference was so strong when together, it was difficult to imagine that wherever they went it wouldn't remain so strong. That would come later. The sons and daughters, Cleary guessed, would remember it as a dream is remembered.

Many were high, or drunk, and there was much dancing, play. Everything they owned was in their trucks, and they traded, made gifts. Some worked on their trucks.

For Cleary, it was what John's funeral should have been.

Ruby should have been there, he thought. She would have liked it. The spirit was her spirit when she let it be.

Cleary wished too that Laura could see it, be there, feel it. She had known the feel of the gatherings at Thorbjorg's, but this was different. They had taken several steps forward. There was the strength of centered energy now.

It went on until the sun went down, when the realities of hunger and crying children and a need for a place to sleep took over. Need, Cleary thought – the female principle.

Which made the male principle excess, he thought. That sounded right, excess and need, expansion and contraction. A man had to have a place to put his energies, had to find a place where they were needed.

"Are you stoned, or what, Cleary?" Bill asked.

Bill had found a girl to take home, a very young girl, Cleary thought, looking at her.

"I was just taking it all in," Cleary said.

Bill and the girl were on his chopper. Big Mike was fussing with his. He couldn't keep it running at slow speeds.

"Where you going to stay?" Bill asked. "You can stay at my place, if you want." He laughed. "Maybe the broad can take care of all of us."

The girl didn't like the sound of it and started to get off, but Bill took hold of her arm. She started to cry.

She wasn't what Bill had in mind. He almost lifted

her off the chopper. "Kids," he said. "They're all kids. Get the fuck out of here!" he yelled.

The girl couldn't keep from yelling back as she ran off. "You dirty old man!"

Bill started the chopper, would have chased her down, if Big Mike hadn't gotten his running, yelled what sounded like a war cry, and peeled rubber. Bill took off, trying to catch him.

Mike was in the oncoming lane when they hit the curve at the far end of the street, Bill passing on his right. There was nowhere for the truck coming toward them to go. It stayed in its lane, and the truck and the chopper crashed head on.

From where he stood, Cleary watched Mike leave the chopper, lift into the air. There was a point at which he saw the tension go out of Mike's body.

Cleary ran toward the crash. He's dead, Cleary thought. He has to be dead.

No one was so hurt in the truck that they couldn't get out. They had seen the body fly over them. They knew whoever it was would be hurt, or dead, and felt they had to find him.

Bill was enough ahead of Mike that he wasn't certain what had happened, until he glanced back. He too saw Mike in the air. Like Cleary, he knew Mike was dead. He slowed, turned, rolled slowly back.

Mike's body was on the edge of the road. Those from the truck reached it as Bill did, but seeing him, stood back out of his way. Bill dismounted, knelt beside Mike. His yell was pure rage.

Big Mike's funeral was a statement.

The bikers had always been there, part of what the public saw happening in the Haight-Ashbury. They were assumed to be one with all the others in the area.

The connection was there on the surface – the two groups did occupy the same space. Down deep, there was also the same disrespect for hierarchy, the same knowledge that those in power were in power because, however subtle and manipulative, they pushed people around. And all on the street understood that power extended only so far as it could be enforced.

The country, the world, had become the playground for the power structures, and whether their ideological bases were economic or religious, they were never more than interpretations of a reality all might consider for themselves. It was naive to accept any of it on faith, to accept any of it but what you yourself found workable.

The degree to which you played in a game you yourself hadn't devised determined your allegiance, your tribe, your life. But all had to agree, ultimately, that the natural laws that lie beneath it all, the natural world and the destinies it would certainly hand you, were there, however much you might forget them, whichever game you might play. They alone described the perimeters you were forced to work or play within.

How you understood those natural laws – whether or not you were comfortable with them, had accepted their inevitability, their functioning, or whether you ignored them, also determined your life.

Most in the Haight, Cleary thought, most who had left Thorbjorg's for caravans and communes, grew to maturity separated from the natural world. For them it was an idea, an abstraction, which might be beautiful, or fearsome, but it had nothing tangible to do with them, until, at some unknown point, it rudely intersected their lives.

Most of the bikers, on the other hand, had come

from families, like Bill's, who had an intimate and ongoing relationship with survival. Whether from a city or the land, they knew that there was a very real border that you had to live with, a border you might edge up to, had at times to edge up to, but it was a border that once you crossed you would never cross again. There was nothing abstract about it. And because they always knew it was there, it would never intersect their lives as it might the lives of the others. They would merge with it, join it.

Like all who have lived with a border, they seemed to know better, and feared less, what they would find on the other side.

Cleary saw the statement Mike's funeral made as having to do with lifestyle. You couldn't assume a lifestyle, it had to be integral and grow out of what the substance was. No matter what it was, it would then be appropriate.

He had liked the sense he'd had of the truck people, but they paled when you saw the bikers. These were the barbarians. This was the tribe that had spread out over the world so long before.

The real thing, Cleary thought. Of course they were all real, but the energies of middle-class kids would dissipate. When they got out there where nobody wanted them the way they were playing it, when they got squeezed and saw how alone they were, their styles would change, they'd become what they had always been. They had the vision, but the vision wasn't enough. It was like money, it would only take you so far.

You had to be locked in. If it wasn't there in who you were, it had to be imposed on you. You couldn't choose to be who you weren't. You grew the way you had to grow, like the branches, Cleary thought. You went the way you wanted to go, unless somebody like Thorbjorg eased you into another direction.

Certain of the ancient Celts mourned their dead by cutting their hair, gashing their bodies, and then breathing the fumes of hemp, or marihuana, that had been thrown over hot coals in a small enclosed space.

Bill and his friends gave their grief the same intense reality.

No one knew how many choppers there were in the procession that moved from Marin, over the Golden Gate Bridge, through northern San Francisco, to the Panhandle, that part of Golden Gate Park that runs parallel to Haight Street, the part of the park where the Diggers gave out free food, and the Grateful Dead and others gave free concerts.

There was no fear of physical harm among the riders. They had rather the Celt's understanding that their bodies would bear new wounds, as the grief they felt and wished to demonstrate demanded it. Their mood was confrontational, and as they moved, police cars and motorcycles all along their route felt justified in being there to safeguard anyone foolish enough to get in their way.

There was no public understanding that what was happening was a righteous observance of timeless beliefs. These were outlaws, all thought, out to make trouble.

Soon after they reached their destination, where the Grateful Dead and countless others from the Haight area joined them, the area was circled off by the police. Cleary was stopped a block from the park, the intersection controlled. They wanted to see his paperwork, looked the truck over, before they allowed him to enter the area.

The Dead's music drew most of those who were there from the Haight, and the music and the presence of people who were there expressly to hear it, helped to keep the gathering orderly. Drugs and alcohol provided most with whatever self-inflicted suffering they needed.

It didn't work for Bill. Bill's father had died. Little John had died. The only woman he had ever really felt good about was gone, on the run, and hadn't even said goodbye. And Mike's death was his fault. If he hadn't been there, on his right, Mike might have gotten out of the way.

Bill couldn't listen to the music. He couldn't talk for more than a few minutes with anyone. Not even Cleary, who had known them all.

Bill walked from one end of the gathering to the other, and back, several times, his bottle in his hand, seeking the tightest groups to jostle through. He was angry. He was being fucked over, and he didn't like it.

All Bill came in contact with, knew him or quickly saw, even in their own states, that the slightest provocation would push him over an edge they didn't want to be on the other side of. Each man knew that unless Bill was killed quickly any attempt would take too many of them as well, and each knew he would be largely alone, there was little agreement among them. That he could find no one to stand up to him angered Bill still more.

Others had worked through their grief, or were at least stoned or drunk, when the Dead went home. Bill's rage was still building. He wasn't ready for it to be over. It wasn't over for him.

On one of his passes, Cleary thought how much Bill's eyes looked like the eyes of an eagle they'd once found wounded and unable to fly. They had thrown a tarp over it, taken it to Bill's, put it in a shed, and nursed it back to health. Then when it first flew, and tore apart a stuffed owl Bill used to hunt crows, Bill killed it.

The choppers began to leave, in small groups, in different directions. Bill was angry that they were leaving. It wasn't time to leave. It wasn't over for him.

He walked from group to group as they made ready, tried to talk them into staying, and when they refused, yelled after them.

When only those few who came so often to Thorbjorg's with him remained, he started his chopper. The others had to hurry to catch him.

As Cleary walked to his truck, he wondered if the police were still there.

Bill saw the police cars in front of him, glanced back, saw that the others were behind him. He accelerated. They could catch up, he must have thought.

There was confusion among the police cars. Some of the officers took cover, others had it in mind to wave him down. He came on them quickly, and they weren't sure he wouldn't stop until he was in the opening between them, moving through. They went for their guns. He was past them when they opened fire.

Bill stayed with the chopper, but lost control, and it crashed into a parked car. He was dead, his body riddled with bullets.

The police found Bill's father's gold watch in his pocket. It was still running.

———————

Cleary wondered if he hadn't seen it all even then, as he might have seen a motion picture – with a distance that had allowed him to survive, when the others didn't. To be, as Thorbjorg had said, the survivor.

Maybe his sense of the possible ways that anything might go had pulled him back from the disasters Thorbjorg predicted, from the disasters behavior and direction project.

Bill's mother came out from Missouri, and Cleary helped her put his things in order. She gave him the gold watch. Bill had no kids, she said.

Bill was cremated, shipped back to Missouri by UPS for burial. Cleary could imagine Frank and Jesse James, on horseback in the timber, watch the green truck drive up to Bill's mother's.

He hadn't counted on it, but Bill would beat him home, Cleary thought.

Neither Little John's nor Bill's death removed them from Cleary's process of projection. They lived in Cleary's mind, like actors in a film still being made, moved again and again with variations through each scene. There were many ways to play those parts, even if you kept them close to the way he remembered them happening. Cleary tried to keep each character consistent, even when he knew he had changed things, fantasized, noted that there were always inconsistencies, as he knew there had been.

He once imagined driving Ruby's wrecked Buick up to where Bill lay, gunned down. He watched himself, Laura and Loup, Ruby, John, Mike, all get out. Even the lamb was there. Bill stood up, dusted himself off. "I was beginning to wonder where everybody was," he laughed.

When Emmett Grogan died, Cleary considered his death. It was too consistent, he thought. Emmett had been the "public" Digger, the man allowed to stand between the others and the media. He often took things into his own hands, often took the media in directions that were his own rather than the group's. His self-interest became the focus of media attention. Media created him as they thought, for their purposes, he ought to be, without the inconsistencies all who knew him knew he had. His death was a media death, a death one might have created for him from his media image. It was reported he died on the last train from Coney Island on April Fool's day from an overdose.

It didn't always happen as you thought it might. The possibilities were endless, Cleary thought, and for Thorbjorg, realities even before she came to them.

Raymond, Cleary's cousin, pointed out the clearing where Cleary built himself a cabin. It was close to Raymond's house, but out of sight. Cleary built the place in six weeks. There was one room and a porch. He was not far from his folks.

A woman called several times during the winter. Cleary had no phone, and the calls came to Raymond's. Cleary never talked about the woman who called, and Raymond never asked.

The following spring, Cleary left. He would go visit Laura, he said, then drive through the south to the east coast, check out Maine. A friend, Big Mike, had once told him it was a great place, and he wanted to see it for himself.

Raymond was sorry to see him go. He would miss the boy too. Egil wasn't much younger than his own kids, and Dee had fit him right in. He was sure they'd be back. They had a cabin now. Someday he and Cleary would teach Egil and his own boys all the words to "Jesse James."